JOSEPH OF ARIM
AND JESUS

"Unto Levi is given the priesthood,
and unto Judah the kingdom ...."

The Testament of the Twelve Patriarchs, the Sons of Jacob

A Bold and Enlightening Presentation of Research Findings about Joseph of Arimathea and Jesus,
as well as a Genealogical and Historical Investigation into Their Shared Priestly and Royal Ancestry,

Researched and Written by

ROBERT H. NELSON AND EMMA L. NELSON

RHN
AND
ELN

Joseph of Arimathea and Jesus
Researched and Written by Robert H. Nelson and Emma L. Nelson

JOSEPHofARIMATHEAandJESUS@gmail.com

ISBN-13: 978-1514226599
ISBN-10: 1514226596

Library of Congress Control Number: 2015909485

CreateSpace Independent Publishing Platform
North Charleston, SC, USA

Printed by CreateSpace, an Amazon company

This book is dedicated to the memory of
Bertha Happy Gans (1879-1968).

Bertha Happy Gans
was a direct descendant of
Joseph of Arimathea, as well as
Aaron (the great-grandson of Levi), and
David (the eighth great-grandson of Judah),
through her mother (Dorcas Rebecca Colvin Goe),
and, in addition, through her father (John Heaton Gans).

A Message from the Authors…

The name "Joseph of Arimathea" refers to a specific person in history, and the name implies that he was from a city called Arimathea. That full name was used in the Bible, so it has been assumed to be accurate.

It is possible, however, that Arimathea was not even a city at all (contrary to the statement in Luke 23:51), or became a known place only after Joseph built an estate there. It is certain that his original name was Yehosef bar Matthat with bar meaning "son of" in Aramaic, which was the dialect of the Hebrew language that Jesus spoke. The Joseph who is the subject of this book was a son of Matthat whose ancestry is shown in Luke 3:24-34. Male names in that period of history, and in Aramaic, followed this naming pattern: the given name, then bar, then the name of the father.

Therefore, his name indicated that he was Yehosef, and he was a son of Matthat. Presumably the original form of the name, Yehosef bar Matthat, morphed into more recognizable forms (Joseph bar Matthat, Joseph bAr mathea, and then to Joseph of Arimathea) over the latter decades of the first century A.D. when the gospels were written in Greek, and later when the gospels were translated into Latin and then into English.

We will use the name "Joseph of Arimathea" throughout this book because it is the name widely understood today to designate the individual we are writing about here. It has been established as the accepted name by its usage in all four of the gospels that were later included in the Bible.

Robert H. Nelson and Emma L. Nelson

Contents

Notes

Preface

Joseph of Arimathea was a real person. In fact, he was a giant of history. A few recent "new age" pseudohistory authors have erroneously written in numerous books that Joseph of Arimathea was one and the same with James, the brother of Jesus. Actually, Joseph of Arimathea was the great-uncle of James, just as he was the great-uncle of Jesus. (Yes, that also makes Mary the mother of James, but in a second marriage after the death of Joseph "the carpenter.") The fabrication, presented by those "new age" authors, with no evidence, required a lie that their death dates were the same, even though it is well known and accepted that James was killed in A.D. 62, and that Joseph of Arimathea died a natural death in A.D. 82. James never left Jerusalem, at least not as an adult. Joseph of Arimathea never returned to Jerusalem after running for safety from the Jews, as he protected the family and friends of Jesus, most importantly in A.D. 35 and then for many years thereafter. The "new age" authors should have classified their books as fiction, but then, that would have hurt their sales of books to people thirsting for the truth.

Why did we research and write here about Joseph of Arimathea? After all, he was a man who has been the subject of numerous biographical statements over the centuries, some basically true, and some outright lies. We became acquainted with him when we included him as one of the "Famous Ancestors" in our earlier book entitled *From Great Men: The Famous Ancestors of Alice de Plumpton,* which was published in 2012 in a print edition and also as an eBook. As genealogists, as well as historians, we recognize that Joseph of Arimathea is quite unusual in that his ancestry can be accurately presented even after two millennia, largely because of his family ties to Jesus, but also because he was a Prince of David himself. He had connections, which were widely known, to some of the most famous ancestral lines in all of history. We felt that, as researchers and authors, we should further investigate the life and ancestry of this man of God who has influenced and touched all of us, whether we know it or not.

We have conducted this investigation around the basic facts that we presented in our earlier book, but we have gone further to develop his story and then present his ancestry for the readers of this book. We have structured this book in three parts, the first being the story of Joseph of Arimathea and Jesus, which also includes additional research findings and a genealogical chart showing a descent line from Joseph into modern times. The second part discusses the priestly ancestry of Joseph of Arimathea and Jesus, which includes Aaron, the first High Priest of Israel. In that second part we include a genealogical chart showing a descent line from Aaron down to Joseph of Arimathea and Jesus, and we show how the non-royal descent line of Joseph of Arimathea and Jesus from David, through Nathan, connects with their line from the High Priests. The third part of this book covers the royal ancestry of Joseph of Arimathea and Jesus, which includes the kings of Judah. We also include in part three a genealogical chart showing a descent line from David, through Solomon, down through the good king, Josiah, and then on down to Joseph of Arimathea and Jesus. In that same chart we also show the Davidic line through the Irish and Scottish kings and then on into modern times.

This is a book of careful research, with numerous notes for each part presented following Section 9. This book also contains a selected bibliography and a comprehensive index. Of course, it is not possible to know the complete detailed story of two individuals who lived two thousand years ago. We have used trusted sources, though, which add a great amount of information to the limited statements which appear in the four gospels about Joseph of Arimathea and his involvement with Jesus. Unlike the "new age" authors we do not present outlandish claims for the reader to be amazed by. Our goal has simply been to get to the truth, and that truth will simply amaze you.

While some may believe, after reading this book, that we are heretics as far as Christianity is concerned, we must point out that many early followers of Jesus were also labeled as heretics, and many of them were killed because they did not agree with the dogma which was developing in the early Church. The matter of what is heresy and what is orthodoxy is quite interesting to consider. If many of the early followers of Jesus, including the descendants of the family of Jesus, did not agree with Paul's vision of Christianity, was not the belief of Paul and his followers the actual heresy? Was not the belief of someone like Joseph of Arimathea (who, unlike Paul, knew Jesus personally) and the belief of each descendant of the family of Jesus the actual orthodoxy? We assert in this book that Jesus, himself, would be considered a heretic today since his beliefs would have been in conflict with the basic tenets of what Christianity ultimately became. In fact, Jesus would have condemned Christianity at its beginning, just as his brother, James, had a problem with the beliefs and practices of the developing Church which was outside the Jerusalem Nazarene synagogue community and tailored to attract the uncircumcised masses of the Roman Empire.

One other feature of this book that the reader will encounter is the investigation into the religion and Israelite ethnicity of Jesus which gives an insightful analysis of a topic which is unknown or misunderstood by most people. You will be shocked when you learn our conclusions.

Much of the material in this book is not widely known. The facts and conclusions that are presented here may be difficult for some to accept since they differ from what many were taught to believe.

On a personal note, we feel that we both know Joseph of Arimathea as a close friend and religious mentor since we have thought so much about him for such a long period of time, and since we are in such awe of him. We believe that his wish for each of us, author and reader alike, would be that every one of us is able to experience the kingdom of God that he, himself, so eagerly awaited.

Part One

Joseph of Arimathea and Jesus

"… Joseph of Arimathea, being a disciple of Jesus, but secretly for fear of the Jews …"[1]

The Gospel of John

Section 1
Joseph of Arimathea and Jesus
(Including Additional Research Findings)

Joseph of Arimathea is most commonly known because of the biblical references to his role in providing a tomb for Yeshua. (Throughout this book we will refer to Yeshua as Jesus, which is the Hellenized form of the Hebrew name in the Aramaic dialect, and the form that is most recognized today.)[2] However, very few details about Joseph are included in the Bible, so it has been necessary to conduct extensive research to find out more about this extraordinary man. From the factual information that has been discovered a biographical sketch emerges.

Joseph of Arimathea was the son of Matthat[3] and his second wife, Rachel. He was a direct descendant of Aaron, who was the first High Priest of Israel and the older brother of Moses.

See "A Genealogical Chart Showing a Descent Line From Aaron to Joseph of Arimathea and Jesus" in Section 6, page 57.

Joseph of Arimathea was also directly descended from King David and he was referred to as a Prince of David.

See "A Genealogical Chart Showing a Descent Line From David, Through Solomon (to Joseph of Arimathea and Jesus)" in Section 9, page 87.

He was, therefore, a direct descendant of both the first High Priest of Israel and the greatest king of Judah and Israel, as well as a direct descendant of both Levi and Judah, the founders of two of the Twelve Tribes of Israel. Joseph of Arimathea was, therefore, of Israelite descent. (See "What is the difference between an Israelite and a Jew?" in *Additional Research Findings* later in this section.)

Joseph of Arimathea was married to a woman named Alyuba, and they had at least two children, a daughter Anna and a son Josephes.[4] Joseph of Arimathea has descendants living today.

See "A Genealogical Chart Showing a Descent Line From Joseph of Arimathea into Modern Times" in Section 3, page 41.

His much older half-brother, Heli (the name is linguistically the same as Joachim), was the father of Mary and the grandfather of Jesus. Joseph of Arimathea was, therefore, the great-uncle of Jesus.[5] He assumed a larger role with Jesus after Joseph "the carpenter" died during the early childhood of Jesus.

Joseph of Arimathea was a prominent and extremely wealthy member of society. The high regard with which he was held is revealed by the title, "Marmore," that was used to refer to him and which means great lord. He was the Roman Minister of Mines who was in charge of the mining and trading of metals, and he owned the ships used to transport those raw materials. Tin and lead were the valued metals of those times, and Joseph was in a position to influence the movement of those metals throughout the Mediterranean area, and from mines in Cornwall and Somerset in Britain to other areas in the Roman Empire. Joseph himself traveled widely and had influential contacts far beyond his place of birth, especially in Britain where he was known and highly respected by King Arviragus,[6] a Druid King of Siluria, and his royal family. Joseph of Arimathea was also a member of the Sanhedrin,[7] the ruling council that was situated in Jerusalem.

Joseph of Arimathea was a very pious individual, and was one of the Essene brethren, and possibly the leader of an Essene colony near Jerusalem.[8] Jesus and his immediate family were, most likely, also of the Essene brethren and shared the Essene beliefs.[9] During this time in history and in this region the dominant religion was Judaism, and it was composed of four major sects, in addition to many smaller sub-sects.

Certain general beliefs of Judaism were common to all of those groups. They believed in the omnipotence of one God, the creator of everything. They believed that certain individuals were prophets, who were given insight from God and were able to prophesy future events. They believed that the greatest of those prophets was Moses, and that God had imparted unto Moses the laws which all people must follow. They believed that those instructions which were inscribed in the Torah were the Word of God. The people believed that a king of Israel, the Messiah, would emerge from the line of David through Solomon, as prophesied. They believed that the Messiah would be a powerful military leader who would save them from their Roman oppression and bring peace. They did not believe that the Messiah would be divine. Most of the people believed in resurrection, not only in terms of an individual's life after death, but as the ultimate triumph of good over evil.

The four main sects of Judaism during the time of Joseph of Arimathea were the Pharisees, the Sadducees, the Zealots, and the Essenes. Those groups all shared basic beliefs, but had areas of disagreement over specific beliefs and practices.

The Pharisees made up the largest group.[10] There were many diverse types of Pharisees, but they all believed in the strict adherence to the oral law and

The following citations are from the King James Version:

> "When the even was come there came a rich man of Arimathea, named Joseph, who also himself was Jesus' disciple: He went to Pilate, and begged the body of Jesus. Then Pilate commanded the body to be delivered. And when Joseph had taken the body, he wrapped it in a clean linen cloth, And laid it in his own new tomb, which he had hewn out in the rock: and he rolled a great stone to the door of the sepulchre, and departed."[16]

> "Joseph of Arimathea, an honorable counseller, which also waited for the kingdom of God, came, and went in boldly unto Pilate, and craved the body of Jesus. And Pilate marvelled if he were already dead: and calling unto him the centurion, he asked him whether he had been any while dead. And when he knew it of the centurion, he gave the body to Joseph. And he brought fine linen, and took him down, and wrapped him in the linen, and laid him in a sepulchre which was hewn out of a rock, and rolled a stone unto the door of the sepulchre."[17]

> "And, behold, there was a man named Joseph, a counseller; and he was a good man, and a just: (The same had not consented to the counsel and deed of them;) he was of Arimathea, a city of the Jews: who also himself waited for the kingdom of God. This man went unto Pilate, and begged the body of Jesus. And he took it down, and wrapped it in linen, and laid it in a sepulchre that was hewn in stone, wherein never man before was laid."[18]

> "And after this Joseph of Arimathea, being a disciple of Jesus, but secretly for fear of the Jews, besought Pilate that he might take away the body of Jesus: and Pilate gave him leave. He came therefore, and took the body of Jesus."[19]

Those who followed Jesus' teachings became known as the Followers of the Way, or the Nazarenes. (The word Nazarene comes from a Hebrew word which means descendant of Jesse, the father of David.)

During the period of time following the crucifixion the Followers of the Way were in grave danger, and many had to flee to seek safety. That was especially true because of repeated attacks by Saul of Tarsus who was intent on intimidating and physically harming any identified supporters of this new group.

Joseph of Arimathea used his influence, wealth, and contacts to provide protection for some of the closest supporters and family members of Jesus. Together they traveled to Caesarea, an active seaport on the Mediterranean coast, about seventy miles northwest of Jerusalem. It was a location of relative safety, which depended upon the security provided by the Roman officials ruling at the time.

Joseph, although having some degree of security stemming from his position as a Roman minister, had himself become a target of the Sanhedrin because of his overt actions on behalf of Jesus and his family after the crucifixion. Ultimately Joseph of Arimathea and his companions, whom he was protecting, were apprehended in Caesarea by Jewish extremists and forced out to sea in a boat having neither sails nor oars.[20]

There were thirteen passengers who accompanied Joseph. Those included Lazarus and his sisters, Mary Magdalene and Martha; Salome; as well as Mary, the wife of Cleophas (Alpheus),[21] who was the mother of Jesus, and who had been protected by Joseph of Arimathea for some time. (See "Mary Cleophas" in *Additional Research Findings* in this Section for information showing that Mary, the wife of Cleophas, was the same person as Mary, the mother of Jesus.)

As mentioned previously, the gospels provide information about Joseph's involvement with Jesus at the time of the crucifixion, but they do not relate details of Joseph's life before or after that. One of the most respected sources of information pertaining to Joseph of Arimathea's departure from Caesarea is *Annales Ecclesiastici,*[22] a history written by Caesar Baronius during the years 1588 to 1607. Cardinal Baronius was an Italian historian and Librarian of the Vatican near the end of the sixteenth century. He was asked by Roman Catholic Church leaders to write a history to counter the prominent church history of that era which had been written by Lutheran scholars and was entitled *Magdeburg Centuries.* Baronius, even though he was known as an extreme papal apologist, is renowned for his honest efforts to provide truthful and unbiased information in his monumental history. Baronius, in referring to his history, said: "I have been most careful to guard against obscuring the pure truth by putting in anything doubtful."[23] Baronius' history included an account of Joseph's forced trip by boat.[24]

The Jewish extremists who put Joseph and his companions out to sea lacked the authority to sentence them to death and felt that was a means of placing their fate in God's hands, a fate which would seem to be death. However, the boat reached land, most likely because of assistance rendered by seamen who knew Joseph and followed covertly in other vessels. Joseph's boat landed in Cyrene, a Mediterranean seaport located in what is now Libya. The travelers refitted their ship and continued on across the Mediterranean Sea, landing at Crete, Sicily, near Rome, and then Marseilles.[25]

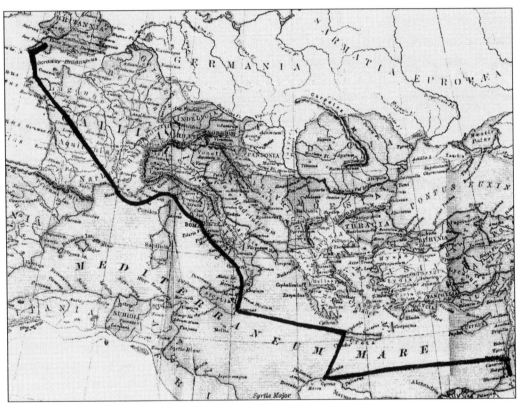

This map was modified by the authors to show the journey of Joseph of Arimathea in A.D. 35 from Caesarea to the Isle of Avalon.[26]

From Marseilles Joseph of Arimathea and most of his companions set out towards Britain. Britain was considered by Joseph to be the safest place in the known world to avoid persecution by either the Romans or the Jews. They traveled up the Rhone and then by land across Gaul on a route familiar to Joseph from his previous tin trading trips. This thirty-day journey through Gaul included a stop at Limoges.

They arrived in Brittany at Morlaix, then boarded sailing vessels and crossed the body of water now known as the English Channel to Cornwall. From there they traveled overland approaching the Isle of Avalon.[27] Then they boarded small boats to reach the island.

(The Isle of Avalon, now known as Glastonbury, England, is no longer an island.)

That part of the journey would have been especially treacherous since it was not a part of the familiar trading route.

After traveling more than twenty-five hundred miles from Caesarea they were welcomed at the Isle of Avalon by King Arviragus, who presented each of the twelve individuals arriving with a large plot of land. That land would remain tax free in perpetuity, as is verified in the *Domesday Book* which was compiled for William the Conqueror and completed in the year 1086.[28] The tax free status of the gifts of land confirms the existence of the ancient religious organization that existed in Glastonbury, that which was led initially by Joseph of Arimathea.

> "Domus Dei in magno Glaston. monasterio quod secretum Domini vocatur, Ecclesia Glaston. habet in itsa villa xii. hydas quae nunquam geldaverunt."[29]

> ("The Domus Dei, in the great monastery of Glastingbury, called the Secret of the Lord. This Glastingbury church possesses, in its own villa, xii. hides of land which have never paid tax.")[30]

Joseph of Arimathea had been asked by the apostle Philip to establish a place of worship in Britain where descendants there of the Tribes of Israel could be introduced to the teachings of Jesus. This was consistent with the request of Jesus that his followers spread his message among the Israelites: "These twelve Jesus sent forth, and commanded them, saying, Go not into the way of the Gentiles, and into any city of the Samaritans enter ye not: But go rather to the lost sheep of the house of Israel."[31]

It is clear that Jesus was telling his disciples to limit their contact to the Israelites who were the twelve tribes that came down from Jacob's sons. This excluded the Jews, meaning those non-Israelite, mixed ancestry people living in Judea, and the Gentiles who were not descended from the twelve tribes.

Eventually Joseph of Arimathea established a Nazarene synagogue to carry out that mission. A primitive building was constructed in which they could praise God and practice their beliefs. Of course, the teachings of Jesus were an integral part of the worship services, especially those ideas included in the Sermon on the Mount.[32] The teachings of the Nazarene synagogue were epitomized by this triad which was written by Lazarus and quoted at that time:

> "Believe in God who made thee; Love God who saved thee; Fear God who will judge thee."[33]

Joseph of Arimathea was an inspiring figure, and he had a powerful message about seeking the kingdom of God. The Druids welcomed his information and insights. Joseph was able to give a first-hand account of the teachings of Jesus. While Joseph was establishing a worship place in Britain, James, the brother of Jesus, had become the leader of the Nazarenes back in Jerusalem. There would, undoubtedly, have been communication (though limited and difficult) between James and Joseph of Arimathea, especially since James' mother was one of those who had accompanied Joseph and was living on the Isle of Avalon. Joseph was very successful in providing protection for those who had fled to the Isle of Avalon with him, and he was successful in converting many of the Britons to his Hebrewism beliefs which by then included the teachings of Jesus. Joseph's ministry in Britain would have been very similar to the work of James back in Jerusalem. However, the basic beliefs that both men espoused were being challenged by another person, one who falsely claimed to be an apostle of Jesus. That person was Paul of Tarsus. (Judas was replaced by Matthias, not Paul, to be the twelfth apostle.)[34]

Though Joseph of Arimathea was far removed geographically from James and his conflicts with Paul, it appears that he was still impacted by Paul's increasing influence. Joseph had been appointed by Philip, his dear friend, to teach among the Britons. However, Paul knew that Joseph of Arimathea's message about the teachings of Jesus conflicted with his own views, and he knew that that message would frustrate his efforts to convert the people of Britain to the Pauline beliefs. So he found it necessary to send devoted followers to carry his own ideas to the Britons. Those were followed by others in later years, and Paul's views and teachings ultimately prevailed over the Nazarene message that Joseph of Arimathea had spread, although not completely for several centuries.

Joseph of Arimathea lived peacefully in Britain for many years. In A.D. 82 Joseph died,[35] and he was buried in the ancient synagogue on the Isle of Avalon. According to Maelgwyn, an uncle of Saint David, writing about A.D. 540,[36] Joseph of Arimathea was buried over the burial plot of Mary, the mother of Jesus.[37]

Joseph of Arimathea and his companions on the Isle of Avalon had avoided the very tragic and brutal treatment that befell the many disciples and relatives of Jesus who served throughout the Roman Empire. Almost all of the followers of Jesus who had scattered to spread his word met violent deaths. In fact, the Desposyni, the descendants of the close family members of Jesus, continued to be oppressed for many generations.

Joseph of Arimathea is known mostly for his biblical role in providing a tomb for Jesus, but he impacted history in other ways as well. He provided protection and safe passage for some of Jesus' closest followers and family members during the dangerous period following the crucifixion. He also spread the teachings of Jesus to the descendants of the Israelites living in Britain, some of whom carried that message throughout Gaul and even to Rome itself before Paul had first arrived there.[38]

Before his death[39] (about fifty years after the crucifixion of Jesus), Joseph of Arimathea would have become aware that the teachings of his great-nephew, Jesus, had been largely eliminated from the growing movement by Paul and his followers, who stressed instead the teachings about the mystical figure called the Christ that had been invented by Paul, using pagan influences. Paul's entire movement was demeaning to the historical Jesus, and to God, and if Jesus had witnessed it he would have been outraged. Much of that developing religion, Christianity, was based on Paul's teachings that the laws of God were to be rejected, and that the most significant requirement was acceptance, on faith, of the Christ figure. Christianity dismissed the actual religion of Jesus, and later even condemned it.

Obviously, Joseph of Arimathea and Jesus, both being Torah-observant, would not have accepted the religion that became known as Christianity. Joseph of Arimathea believed in Jesus because of his life. The later Christians believed in Jesus because of his death.

Joseph of Arimathea would have known that he had done his best to spread the true message of Jesus. Being descended from Aaron of the priestly line from Levi, and from David, the first king in the line from Judah, both Joseph of Arimathea and Jesus were Israelites and of the religion of Hebrewism, or the Religion of the Old Testament. Today, ironically, Joseph of Arimathea and Jesus are almost always thought to be connected only to Christianity. It is clear, though, that no religion built around the beliefs and actions of Paul would have been acceptable to them.

Additional Research Findings

The Virgin Birth of Jesus

Many of the beliefs that are now included in Christian doctrine were not beliefs held by the contemporaries of Jesus, but were added long after his crucifixion. The earliest biblical inclusion of the virgin birth of Jesus was in the Gospel of Matthew which was written about A.D. 85, and later included in the Bible. Matthew (or most probably a later translator or reviser) stated:

> "Behold, a virgin shall be with child, and shall bring forth a son, and they shall call his name Emmanuel, which being interpreted is, God with us."[40]

Matthew was trying to use a prophecy of Isaiah to show that Isaiah was speaking about the birth of Jesus, but actually Isaiah was speaking about a child to be born in the 8th century B.C., a future heir of King Ahaz of Judah. Isaiah used the Hebrew word "almah" which means "young woman," but when the attempt was made to utilize that prophecy and write it in Greek, the Hebrew word "almah" was incorrectly translated as "virgin" instead of the correct words "young woman."

(Isaiah 7:14 in The Holy Scriptures According to the Masoretic Text does not use the word "virgin."[41] The Christian compilers of the King James Version made sure that Isaiah 7:14 included the word "virgin" in order to completely carry out their plot to deceive.)

In an earlier Gospel of Matthew which was written in Hebrew sometime prior to A.D. 62,[42] he did not include the word "virgin." The exact quote in Matthew 1:23 from the book *Hebrew Gospel of Matthew* by Professor George Howard is:

> "Behold the young woman is conceiving and will bear a son and you will call his name Emmanual, that is, God with us."[43]

So the inclusion of the word "virgin" in the later Matthew Gospel written in Greek is how the virgin birth story was first introduced, and then it was used to promote the proposition that Jesus was divine.

The Divinity of Jesus

In keeping with his religious beliefs, Joseph of Arimathea would have viewed Jesus as an extraordinary and inspired man but definitely not a divine being. One of the basic tenets of Hebrewism was the oneness of God. To believe that a human was also divine would have been considered idolatrous. A man could not be God, and likewise God could not be a man. "God is not a man ...."[44] Jesus himself stated: "The first of all the commandments is, 'Hear, O Israel: The Lord our God is one Lord ....'"[45, 46]

The deification of Jesus became a part of Christian doctrine many years later. The Apostles Creed, which is believed to have originated during the late second century, does not include any explicit mention of the divinity of Jesus. It was not until the Council of Nicaea in A.D. 325 that the divine nature of Jesus became an official part of Christian doctrine.

Jesus as the Messiah

Many of Jesus' followers considered him to be the Messiah, but Joseph of Arimathea would not have believed that. Joseph of Arimathea would have been intimately aware of his shared genealogy with Jesus, and he would have realized that the ancestry of Jesus did not satisfy all of the hereditary criteria which the prophecies deemed necessary for an individual to qualify to be the Messiah.

It is true that Jesus was descended from David in his father's (Joseph "the carpenter") direct male line. (That is, if Joseph "the carpenter" was the actual human father of Jesus.) And it is true that the descent from David was through Solomon in line with prophecy.[47] But it is also true that Jeconiah was in his male line going back to David.[48]

So Jesus descended from David through Jeconiah, and prophecy mandated that no descendant of Jeconiah could ever sit on the throne of David and rule as the Messiah.[49]

(Of course, since the Christian messiah, or Christ, existed because of Paul's invention, there was no need for it to be an accurate fulfillment of Old Testament prophecy.)

The Trinity

At the time of Jesus the concept of the Trinity had not yet been created. It is certain, though, that Joseph of Arimathea and Jesus would not have believed in it.

The concept of the Trinity developed over a period of time to become a doctrine that is now mandatory for a Christian. The Trinity had not evolved up to the fourth century, but under the rule of the Roman emperor Constantine, many beliefs were grafted on to the already compromised religion which had by then completely adapted to the Gentile environment and had become corrupted by paganism.

The term Trinity does not appear in the New Testament, and the followers of Jesus would never have heard of it. Joseph of Arimathea and his fellow believers of the first century, including Jesus, would have considered the doctrine of the Trinity to be blasphemous and against their monotheistic beliefs. (For more information see "The Great Commission of Christianity" on pages 33-36 in the *Additional Research Findings* in this Section.)

The Assumption of Mary

Mary, the mother of Jesus, was known while a young girl by her Hebrew name, Miriam. However, she is most often known and recognized today by the name Mary. Mary was the daughter of Heli[50] and his wife, Anna.

Mary traveled with her uncle, Joseph of Arimathea, to the Isle of Avalon in Britain in A.D. 35.[51] She lived out her life in that protected and relatively safe environment, died a natural death in A.D. 48,[52] and was buried in the primitive synagogue on the Isle of Avalon.[53]

Mary, the mother of Jesus, was drawn by Leonardo da Vinci.[54]

Many people view the later life of Mary as a great mystery. Over the years there have been empty tombs discovered in various places which were said to be Mary's and were purported to prove that Mary was assumed, both body and soul, into heaven. That was a tradition for many years, but there is no actual reference to the Assumption of Mary in the Bible, and the idea was condemned as heretical by two popes, Pope Gelasius in the fifth century and Pope Hormisdas in the sixth century. However, the tradition continued, and since the seventh century the belief in the bodily Assumption of Mary was allowed, even though the Vatican has been aware since that time of the likelihood that Mary was actually buried in Britain on the Isle of Avalon.

In November of 1950, Pope Pius XII declared in the decree *Munificentissimus Deus*[55] that the Assumption of Mary is a dogma of the Roman Catholic Church and threatened that, since it was then a required belief, any dissenter is an apostate who has fallen away completely from the Church and loses salvation.[56] That formalization of what had previously been only a tradition discouraged investigations that would weaken the Church's position.

Admitting Mary's burial in Britain and, before that, her participation in spreading her knowledge of the true beliefs of Jesus would contradict what had become a fundamental belief of Roman Catholicism, that being that Mary had returned to Earth many times in the last two thousand years.

But Mary did live and die as any other human being would. In the Bible Mary was mentioned only one time after the crucifixion of Jesus. That was when she joined the disciples in the Upper Room for prayer.[57]

After that she disappeared from the gospels. The reason for that is not that she had been assumed into heaven, but that she had moved away with other family members and supporters of Jesus, staying at Caesarea for a while and then enduring the lengthy trip all the way to the Isle of Avalon in Britain, where she lived until her death.[58]

Paul of Tarsus

Paul, previously known as Saul, had been among those who persecuted the followers of Jesus. About the year A.D. 37, Paul proclaimed himself to have become a supporter of Jesus. James and the other followers of Jesus were wary of Paul, who had been their enemy, and as Paul became more deeply involved with them it became apparent that his mission was different than theirs.

Eventually a rift developed among the supporters of Jesus. Some continued to follow the Law of Moses while embracing the teachings of Jesus, as James and Joseph of Arimathea did. Others began to follow Paul and accept his teachings as they were presented to the Gentiles. Those teachings included an emphasis on the sacrificial nature of the death of Jesus and the supremacy of faith over good works, unlike James' (the brother of Jesus) belief in good works and not just in faith. This was because Paul could relate to the evil of mankind since he was an admittedly evil individual himself. "For the good that I would I do not: but the evil which I would not, that I do."[59] Jesus had warned his disciples to beware of false prophets who would replace his teachings with their own. "Beware of false prophets, which come to you in sheep's clothing, but inwardly they are ravening wolves."[60] Paul was the type of false prophet that Jesus warned would be changing his beliefs and teachings and forming a belief system that he (Jesus) would not have approved of.

The message of Jesus was for everyone to keep the commandments of God.[61] Paul encouraged the Gentiles not to follow God's laws.[62] That is the greatest example of the false teachings of Paul and his followers, and Jesus would have condemned it.

Paul of Tarsus was the individual who was actually responsible for the founding and growth of what became known as Christianity. Modern Christianity is based largely on Paul's vision and interpretations.

What began as an effort by Jesus to bring back Hebrewism for the descendants of the earlier Israelites became a religion for Gentiles because of Paul's powerful influence. Paul, while named Saul, had been a persecutor of the Nazarenes, those who had followed Jesus and those who joined the group after his crucifixion.

Paul in Romans said "Salute Herodion my kinsman."[63] That proves an admitted bloodline tie to the Herod family. Also, that shows him to be an Edomite Jew for at least part of his ancestry. While much is not known, and certainly not proven, about the ancestry and relatives of Paul, it is certain that he was well connected to the Herod family since he would have needed a great amount of authority to arrest hundreds, if not thousands, of people in an area that was under military rule.

Paul claimed to have known Jesus from a vision and used that association to infiltrate the Followers of the Way, the group who had walked with Jesus, including Jesus' actual family members. That attempt to usurp the belief system away from the followers of Jesus and the family of Jesus resulted in a major power struggle.

(By the time that the gospels were written, twenty years or more after the death of Paul, his views had greatly influenced the gospel writers, thereby posthumously changing the historical record to include his views in place of many of the actual truths.)

Did Paul of Tarsus kill James, the brother of Jesus, in A.D. 62?

As shocking as that may seem to the readers of this book, the authors have discovered a statement of an early Church bishop and historian, Dorotheus, that included the claim that Paul did, indeed, kill James, the brother of Jesus. (Dorotheus was the teacher of Eusebius who was the famous early Church historian.) That statement was included in his book, *The Lives, the Ends, and the Martyrdomes of the Prophetes, Apostles, and seventye Disciples of Our Saviour*,[64] and was reported subsequently as:

> "James, the son of Alpheus, was bishop of Jerusalem by the appointment of the other apostles. He was killed by St. Paul. Having been set by the Jews upon a pinnacle of the temple … Paul thrust him off."[65]

It was also reported about the statement of Dorotheus which concerned the death of James that:

> "Dorotheus, Bishop of Tyrus, who wrote the Lives of the Apostles, says that he was killed by St. Paul."[66]

Another statement which refers to the killing of James by Paul is the following:

> "St. James is said to have been murdered by St. Paul and therefore his death ought not to be laid to the charge of Pagan persecution."[67]

If that is all true, then it is a devastating blow to a central message of Christianity; that is that Paul, after his "conversion," became a different person and then only strived to take the message about his "Christ Jesus" to all the world.

Eusebius seems to try to keep Paul from involvement in the death of James.

> "Eusebius says that 'the Scribes and Pharisees' put him on a wing of the temple, but that upon his testifying in favour of Jesus instead of against him, they began to stone him, and that one of them, a fuller, beat out his brains with the club with which he used to beat clothes."[68]

Dorotheus stated unequivocally that it was Paul who actually pushed James from a pinnacle of the temple to the ground in A.D. 62.[69] It is understandable, though, that Eusebius would have tried to deflect blame from Paul for the murder of James. The Christianity that Eusebius served depended on it.

It appears that possibly Paul was still doing favors for the corrupt High Priests, this time serving as the thug for Ananus, the young and very temporary High Priest. We know that James, the brother of Jesus, had something that Paul could never have. James had a very personal connection to Jesus, being a close half-brother. Also, Paul had a long time animus toward James and had almost killed him many years earlier when he threw him headlong down the steps of the Temple. Following is a description of that earlier confrontation:

> "Then ensued a tumult on either side, of the beating and the beaten. Much blood is shed; there is a confused flight, in the midst of which that enemy [Saul] attacked James, and threw him headlong from the top of the steps; and supposing him to be dead, he cared not to inflict further violence upon him."[70]

While one could understand why Eusebius would have protected Paul by trying to keep the information about Paul's participation in the death of James in A.D. 62 from ever getting out, it is hard to understand why Dorotheus would have stated this fact if it were not true.

The Desposyni

The Desposyni (which means the family of the Lord) were at first highly revered, despite the division that was developing among the supporters of Jesus in regard to following traditional religious laws as encouraged by the Nazarenes, or relaxing those beliefs in order to appeal to the Gentiles as Paul insisted.

After James, the brother of Jesus, was killed in A.D. 62, Simeon succeeded him as the head of the Nazarenes in Jerusalem. Simeon was related to Jesus in two ways. First, he was his cousin, as he was the son of Cleophas, the younger brother of Joseph "the carpenter." Secondly, he was his half-brother, since Mary (the mother of Jesus) had married Cleophas after the death of Joseph "the carpenter" and was the mother of Simeon, as well as James, Joseph, Judas, and at least two daughters.[71] (See "Mary Cleophas" following this in the *Additional Research Findings* in this Section.)

The Nazarenes continued to be led by succeeding generations of the family of Jesus. As time passed, however, the Roman Church felt increasingly threatened by the Desposyni. By the fourth century the teachings of Paul had evolved into the Roman Catholic Church which had become the official religion of the Roman Empire. While basing their newly created religion on Jesus, the Church, ironically, sought to eliminate the very people who were the most intimately related to Jesus, those who had descended from his close family members. Several centuries after the crucifixion the Desposyni had essentially disappeared, most of them having been hunted down and killed by agents of the Roman Catholic Church.

Mary Cleophas

Mary, the mother of Jesus, was married to Cleophas after the death of Joseph "the carpenter." Cleophas was the younger brother of Joseph "the carpenter." The proof of the marriage of Mary, the mother of Jesus, to Cleophas is shown by an examination of the gospel statements about the three women who were looking on at the crucifixion of Jesus.

In <u>Luke</u> it is only reported that women were present.[72]

In <u>Matthew</u> it is stated, "Among which was Mary Magdalene, and Mary the mother of James and Joses, and the mother of Zebedee's children."[73]

In <u>Mark</u> it is stated, "There were also women looking on afar off: among whom was Mary Magdalene, and Mary the mother of James the Less and of Joses, and Salome."[74]

In <u>John</u> it is stated, "Now there stood by the cross of Jesus his mother, and his mother's sister, Mary the wife of Cleophas, and Mary Magdalene."[75]

Pictured are Mary Magdalene, Mary the wife of Cleophas (Mary the mother of Jesus), and Salome.[76]

You can see that <u>Mary Magdalene</u> is included specifically in Matthew, Mark, and John. Then you can see that <u>Mary's sister</u> is included in Matthew, Mark, and John, being described in Matthew as "the mother of Zebedee's children," in Mark as "Salome," and in John as "his [Jesus'] mother's sister." Finally, you can see <u>Mary</u> described in Matthew as "Mary the mother of James and Joses," described in Mark as "Mary the mother of James the Less and of Joses," and described in John as "his [Jesus'] mother." If you combine the statement in Mark about Mary being the mother of James the Less with the statement in John about Mary being the mother of Jesus, you can see that Mary, the mother of James the Less, is also the mother of Jesus.

That leaves in John "Mary the wife of Cleophas." Since there were only three women present in this grouping, "Mary the wife of Cleophas" is obviously a further description of one of the three women involved here.

Since James the Less has been shown above to be the son of Mary, the mother of Jesus,[77] and since James the Less was also known to be the son of Alpheus[78] (the Greek form of the Aramaic name Cleophas), it demonstrates and proves that the person shown as "Mary the wife of Cleophas" was the same person as Mary, the mother of Jesus.

<u>What is the difference between an Israelite and a Jew?</u>

Many books and many scholars say that Judah was the ancestor of the Jews and that the Jews were named for that ancestor. Nothing could be further from the truth.

The name of the geographical place called Judah, which had been named for Judah, the son of Jacob and the great-grandson of Abraham, was the original location of the Tribe of Judah. The name was changed to Judea after the time of the Captivity, which ended about 538 B.C. The English word "Jew" from the Latin "Iudaeus" means Judean, an inhabitant of Judea.[79] The Edomites, who largely populated Judea after the Babylonian Captivity, were called Jews because they resided in Judea. They were not descended from Judah, and they were not called Jews because of him.

The complex and often misunderstood words "Jew," "Jews," and "Jewish," are used today to designate individuals following the religion of "Judaism," or from that heritage. However, these words, as well as the words "Semite," "Hebrew," "Israelite," and "Judahite," have specific connotations.

Abraham, along with his son Isaac and his grandson Jacob, were Hebrews, a word which came from an ancestor of Abraham named Eber. Before Eber the ancestors of Abraham were Semites, being descended from Shem, a son of Noah. Israelites are from Jacob (later given the name Israel by God)[80] beginning with his sons who were the founders of the Tribes of Israel, and their descendants. For example,

Moses and Aaron were Israelites since they were descended from Levi, the founder of the Tribe of Levi and a son of Jacob.

God made a covenant with the Israelites, and they were the ones who were called the chosen people.[81] Judahites are Israelites but specifically the descendants of Judah, the founder of the Tribe of Judah, one of the Tribes of Israel.

The word "Jew" was not used in the entire original text of the Bible, but only in the modern translations and in those the word "Jews" was first used in the book of 2 Kings.[82] As was stated previously, the word "Jew" in the Bible referred to a person from Judea, a region which included people with many different ethnicities, but mainly Edomites.

The term "Jew" was not significant in biblical history until after the remnants of the original descendants of the Tribes of Judah and Benjamin returned following the Babylonian Captivity about 538 B.C. Mixed in with those returning people were many thousands of mixed multitude, or non-Israelite people, who became known as Jews when they then resided in Judea.

Earlier, the lands of the Tribes of Judah and Benjamin had been taken over by Edomites during the Captivity period. Those Edomites were not born of Israelites, but rather were descended from Esau,[83] the brother of Jacob. Many of those later fled to North Africa and then to Spain. Those "Jews" became known as Sephardic Jews and later lived primarily in western Europe.

"In the year B.C. 129, John Hyrcanus conquered the Edomites...the descendants of Esau, who married daughters of Heth, and rather than leave the land they embraced the Jewish religion. After a time, they became absorbed amongst the Jews, and were called Jews; and, as a rule, were not to be distinguished from them. The Jews also mingled with the Canaanites, and during the seventy years' captivity great numbers of them married women of other nations. No doubt these things were done in spite of the wholesome restrictions to which, as a tribe or nation, they felt it their duty to submit. Yet, notwithstanding these violations of the rule, their descendants were known as Jews, not as Edomites or Canaanites."[84]

Many scholars believe that over 90% of all living Jews in the world today are descended from the people of the Turkish-Mongolian tribes of the 8th century called Khazars who lived in what is now southern Russia.

Many of those pagan Khazars adopted Judaism as their religion. They were then considered to be Jews. The Khazars then spread through eastern Europe over the following centuries. Their descendants are called Ashkenazi Jews.

But recent DNA analyses do not agree with those who think that the Ashkenazi Jews did not originate in the Middle East. Several Y-DNA studies have been conducted, and it has been determined that about 75% of all Jewish men (in their male line going back, son to father to father etc.) have ancestry from the Middle East. Jews, except for converts from other ethnicities, do have a common ancestry, and are a distinct population, originating in the Middle East.

The reason is that, according to *The Jewish Encyclopedia*, "the Chazars [Khazars] formerly lived in the mountains of Seir ...."[85] That proves that the earlier ancestors of the Jews were Edomites and that they were descendants of Esau.

> "Thus dwelt Esau in mount Seir: Esau is Edom. And these are the generations of Esau the father of the Edomites in mount Seir ...."[86]

Those Edomites had escaped from the area which was near to what later became Judea, at the time of the destruction of Jerusalem in 587 B.C., and again when Jerusalem, after Judea had become their adopted homeland, was destroyed in A.D. 70. Thus Ashkenazi Jews do have an ancestral connection to the Middle East, that being from Abraham. They do not, however, descend from Israelites.

The article titled "Purity of Race" in *The Jewish Encyclopedia* stated that "some anthropologists are inclined to associate the racial origin of the Jews, not with the Semites, whose language they adopted, but with the Armenians and Hittites of Mesopotamia, whose broad skulls and curved noses they appear to have inherited."[87]

(This information is incorrect, at least in regard to the point that the Jews are not Semites. Being descended from Edomites would make the Jews Semites inasmuch as their ancestor, Esau, was a son of Isaac and a grandson of Abraham, both descendants of Shem. Shem's descendants are Semites.)

Many Jews today claim that they are descended from Israelites, and even King David himself. Some Jews have tried to prove their connection to King David. There is even an organization in Israel whose mission is to help Jews around the world prove their descent from King David.

We have indicated earlier that modern day Jews are not descended from Jacob, so they are not Israelites. They are descended from Jacob's brother Esau, so they are descended from Edomites. Of course, there would be exceptions to that statement, one exception being the many children born of Solomon who dealt with many hundreds of women, many of whom were from foreign lands.[88] So there would be some that were descendants of David even though those Jews would be primarily of Edomite stock.

Present day Jews, even in the unlikely event that they are descended from David as explained above, could not prove descent from David as their only way to prove that would be the usual route through the Rabbis. Trying to prove their descent from David would require them to rely on oral tradition in their families since genealogical records are not there to allow them to prove a complete genealogical line.[89]

It is well known that many Jews at the time of Jesus called for his crucifixion. They did not like the fact that he criticized them for what he saw as the satanic nature of their religion, Judaism. He had many battles with the Pharisees who were Edomite Jews.

When Christianity became a religion of the Gentiles, the gospels included what is now termed an "anti-Semitic bias" against the Jews. That "bias" is believed to be based on the hatred that the Christians thought the Jews displayed towards Jesus. The Christians eventually learned what the Jews thought of Jesus and the Christians by becoming aware of the vile statements included in the Talmud.[90]

The Jews, on the other hand, became obsessed with the statement that appeared in the Gospel of John. Martin Luther's book *On the Jews and Their Lies*,[91] also with vile statements, which was written in 1543, included the following: "'You are of your father the devil.' It was intolerable to them to hear that they were not Abraham's but the devil's children, nor can they bear to hear this today."[92]

And now, four hundred and seventy-two years later, they still can not bear to hear what John reported that Jesus told the Jews, that they were "children of Satan." A posting which appeared as recently as September of 2014 in a blog in the *Jerusalem Post*[93] online indicates that, for the Jews, the statement in the Gospel of John can never be forgiven or forgotten. That full statement in John, which quotes Jesus admonishing the Jews who were descended from Edomites, is as follows:

> "Ye are of your father the devil, and the lusts of your father ye will do. He was a murderer from the beginning, and abode not in the truth, because there is no truth in him. When he speaketh a lie, he speaketh of his own: for he is a liar, and the father of it."[94]

But Jesus did not care that he was insulting people whose ancestry was not pleasing to God, and whose religion (Judaism) was insulting to God.

It is, however, much more understandable that the Jews and the Christians would hate each other forever than that the evangelical Christians would act and donate as if they were Jews themselves.

Many evangelical Christians believe, incorrectly, that the Jews are the "chosen people," and they feel that any people chosen by God should be supported. They believe that the nation God promised to bless[95] refers to the modern state of Israel. If they knew that the modern day Jews are not descendants of the Israelites and thus are not descended from the "chosen people" spoken about in the Bible it is likely they would not be so enamored with the modern state of Israel which is populated by descendants of the Edomites/Khazars, and not by descendants of the Israelites of the Bible.

It is especially surprising that certain highly educated and biblically trained television evangelists, that some refer to as "Christian Zionists," would not know that modern day Jews are not descended from the Israelites. Is it that they are blinded by what they assume to be true?

It is the authors' belief that the modern state of Israel should be supported as the only democracy in the Middle East. We assume, however, that the fanatical support of the modern state of Israel by those "Christian Zionists" mentioned above is based on their incorrect belief that Israelis, and Jews everywhere, are modern day descendants of the Israelites of the Bible.

The Didache

The Didache, or The Teaching of the Twelve Apostles, is possibly dated as early as A.D. 50. It was an instruction manual regarding rituals, the organization of the developing belief system, and ethics.

The Didache was rejected as part of the New Testament, undoubtedly because it did not include any mention of the virgin birth of Jesus, the resurrection, and Jesus as the son of God. In fact it referred to Jesus as a servant of God. It also made clear that the family of Jesus did not consider him to be God.[96]

The Great Commission of Christianity

The Great Commission of Christianity refers to the supposed commission or command that Jesus, after his resurrection, gave to his disciples to include the Gentiles, in order to teach them and to baptize them.

While it is not the primary Bible passage used by Christian apologists to advance The Great Commission of Christianity, there is a statement of Jesus in the Gospel of John that is often quoted to prove their contention that Jesus wanted to include the Gentiles:

> "And other sheep I have which are not of this fold: them also I must bring, and they shall hear my voice; and there shall be one fold, and one shepherd."[97]

The command of Jesus to go only to "the lost sheep of the house of Israel" is not proven to be replaced by this statement in the Gospel of John since the "other sheep" referred to are undoubtedly other Israelites, those of the Northern Tribes as prophesied so precisely in Hosea:

> "Then shall the children of Judah and the children of Israel be gathered together, and appoint themselves one head, and they shall come up out of the land: for great shall be the day of Jezreel."[98]

The Great Commission of Christianity is primarily thought to be authenticated by the statement of Jesus in Matthew 28:19-20 which is believed by most people to include his very specific command:

> "Go ye therefore, and teach all nations, baptizing them in the name of the Father, and of the Son, and of the Holy Ghost: Teaching them to observe all things whatsoever I have commanded you: and, lo, I am with you alway, even unto the end of the world. Amen."[99]

This is a critical Bible passage for the validation of Christianity in that it provides justification for the going out to the Gentiles (all nations) and for baptism to be based on what would be the later Roman Catholic view of the Trinity.

The part of Matthew 28:19-20 in which Jesus is supposedly commanding his disciples to "teach all nations" specifically conflicts with the command by Jesus earlier in Matthew to "Go not into the way of the Gentiles, and into any city of the Samaritans enter ye not: But go rather to the lost sheep of the house of Israel."[100] Jesus is also quoted as saying in Matthew that "I am not sent but unto the lost sheep of the house of Israel."[101]

It seems very clear what Jesus believed and what he wanted, yet Christians make many arguments against the earlier commands of Jesus to say that going to the Gentiles is the new mandatory mission and Jesus is now commanding that to be carried out. How can this be? Scholars through the years have questioned the authenticity of this Commission since it speaks in the language of the Trinity which developed in the fourth century A.D.

Matthew 28:19-20 "in particular only canonizes a later ecclesiastical situation, that its universalism is contrary to the facts of early Christian history, and its Trinitarian formula 'foreign to the mouth of Jesus.'"[102] The answer to that is simple. Traditional Matthew 28:19-20 has been compromised by early translators and scribes. It is necessary to go to a source which has not been changed to agree with the developing Christian doctrine.

The Gospel of Matthew which was written in Hebrew was an earlier writing of Matthew that mysteriously, and suspiciously, disappeared from all Christian hands. Dorotheus, the Bishop of Tyre, knew of it, though, and wrote in his *"Lives of the Apostles"*[103] that:

> "Matthew, the evangelist, wrote the Gospel of our Lord Jesus Christ in the Hebrew tongue, and delivered it unto James, the brother of the Lord according to the flesh, who was bishop of Jerusalem."[104]

That dates the original Gospel of Matthew which was written in Hebrew to sometime prior to A.D. 62 (the year of the murder of James, the brother of Jesus). Most likely it was written about A.D. 50, and possibly as early as A.D. 45.

At least one copy of the Gospel of Matthew which was written in Hebrew was obtained and preserved by certain Jews, thereby allowing it to avoid the manipulation of early (Roman Catholic) Church fathers. The later traditional versions of Matthew in Greek are all flawed. They include the intentional modifications which were used to justify the planned future direction of the Church.

Contrary to the many vehement statements of Christian apologists that have been included in books and articles, and on the internet, the "Shem-Tob" Hebrew text included in the modern book entitled *Hebrew Gospel of Matthew* by Professor George Howard is believed to be originally Hebrew, and not previously translated from either Greek or Latin.[105]

The original Hebrew text used by Professor Howard in his translation avoided modifications during the early years of Christianity, modifications such as those that plagued the Greek scriptures.

It is believed by some biblical scholars that there is convincing evidence that the "Shem-Tob" Hebrew Matthew text is a recension of the actual gospel written by Matthew, himself, in biblical Hebrew. That gospel was subsequently edited over the following centuries without adversely affecting the original text. The "Shem-Tob" Hebrew Matthew text is the closest to the original Gospel of Matthew in Hebrew that is known today.[106]

The Matthew 28:19-20 passages translated into English by Professor Howard for his book *Hebrew Gospel of Matthew* quote Jesus as stating the following:

> "Go and teach them to carry out all the things which I have commanded you forever."[107]

That's it. There is no mention of going to all the nations or the Gentiles, and there is no mention of baptism based on Trinitarian beliefs that are similar to the beliefs of the later Roman Catholic Church.

That is why the apostles knew nothing about a change in the message of Jesus. There was none.

This finding further demonstrates that Jesus, a Torah-observant Israelite, never intended that his message was for any but the Israelites, the lost sheep of the house of Israel.

(See Section 2, pages 37-40, of this book for more information.)

The statement from Matthew 28:19-20 that was translated from the Hebrew by Professor Howard makes clear what the changes were that are now included in the traditional Matthew text that has come down from the Greek.

This is supported by the fact that similar passages in Mark[108] are widely believed by modern scholars to be Christian forgeries. Those passages are a part of the Mark 16:9-20 passages that were added later. Those later additions were not included in two of the earliest Greek manuscripts of the New Testament.[109]

RHN
AND
ELN

Section 2
Jesus: His Religion and Israelite Ethnicity

As was stated in Section 1 of this book (and shown in the chart in Section 6), Jesus was an Israelite. He was a direct descendant of Levi through Aaron.[110] Levi was a son of Jacob. Jacob was named Israel by God.[111] Jesus was also a direct descendant of Judah through David. Judah was also a son of Jacob.[112] Jacob's sons were the first Israelites. Jesus was specifically of Israelite ancestry and ethnicity because he was a direct descendant of two of the sons of Jacob/Israel.[113]

Why then, does everyone say that Jesus was a Jew? Most people think that Jesus was a Jew, but Jesus was an Israelite, not a Jew. Israelites were the ones who were called the chosen people of God.[114] Edomites, and their descendants, now called Jews, are not the chosen people. The fact that modern day Jews want us to think they are descended from Israelites is one of the greatest intentional lies, or misunderstandings, in all of history.

It would be virtually impossible to find a book written about Jesus that doesn't describe him as a Jew. Are they all calling him a Jew because they think he was a Jew by religion? Are they all calling him a Jew because they think he was a Jew by ancestry? A person can be a Jew by religion while not being a Jew by ancestry, and a person can be a Jew by ancestry while not being a Jew by religion. Just what are the facts concerning the religion and ancestry of Jesus?

First, was Jesus a Jew as far as his religion was concerned? No, his religion was Hebrewism; or, as we now call it, the Religion of the Old Testament. That religion was the religion of the Hebrews and the Israelites, and was based on the Law of Moses and the teachings of the prophets. Stephen S. Wise, a former chief rabbi of the United States, said:

> "The return from Babylon [following the Captivity, about 538 B.C.], and the adoption of the Babylonian Talmud, marks the end of Hebrewism, and the beginning of Judaism."[115]

Jesus criticized the Jews, or Pharisees, for establishing Judaism which is based on the Talmud,[116] and which at the time of Jesus was still called the Tradition of the Elders.[117]

When the people returned from Babylon, about 538 B.C., after the Babylonian Captivity, they brought back a different religion than the one practiced just fifty years earlier. The new religion was the Tradition of the Elders (or Judaism), and that religion was based on the teachings of the rabbis rather than the laws of God.

> "Then came to Jesus scribes and Pharisees, which were of Jerusalem, saying, Why do thy disciples transgress the tradition of the elders? for they wash not their hands when they eat bread. But he answered and said unto them, Why do ye also transgress the commandment of God by your tradition?"[118]

In this painting by James Tissot, Jesus was questioned by the Pharisees, and he rebuked them and criticized their religion.[119]

For many years after the return from the Babylonian Captivity, even at the time of Jesus, the remaining Israelites still went to the Temple and participated in the religious activities there. Those Israelites had nowhere else to go, but they tried to hold on to Hebrewism, the religion of their ancestors, even though that religion had been largely eliminated by the rabbis.

Professor Georg Hermann Schnedermann (1852-1917) of the University of Leipzig, a Lutheran theologian, made his point eloquently when he wrote about the two groups at the time of Jesus with different religions and ethnicities.

> He distinguished "between the 'Israelite' and 'Jewish' elements in the intellectual atmosphere in which Jesus grew up: though Judaism reigned in the schools of the scribes and held the field to outward appearance, yet an 'Israelite' strain of piety and conviction prevailed in a certain section of religious society. Those who walked in the green pastures and beside the still waters of this faith of the heart were in touch with the Prophets and understood all that is deepest in the Old Testament."[120]

Many of the people hoped that a leader would emerge who would turn back the clock and allow them to have the religion of God that had disappeared.[121] A mission of Jesus was to give back to the Israelites the religion that had been stolen from them. Definitely, Jesus was not a Jew by religion.

Secondly, was Jesus a Jew by ancestry? Jews were not Israelites as they were not descended from Jacob. They were descended from Esau, the brother of Jacob. While both were grandsons of Abraham and sons of Isaac, Jacob was favored by God.[122] Esau's descendants were called Edomites,[123] and later they were called Jews since many of them were then living in Judea because the Edomites had been captured by John Hyrcanus and forced to convert to the religion then in place in Judea. Jesus stated in Matthew, "I am not sent but unto the lost sheep of the house of Israel."[124] When Jesus sent his disciples out to spread his message he told them, "Go not into the way of the Gentiles, and into any city of the Samaritans enter ye not: But go rather to the lost sheep of the house of Israel."[125] The Jews were not a part of the sheep of the house of Israel that Jesus talked about. Note that it is not the fact that the Jews did not believe in the message of Jesus that made them not of his sheep. Jesus knew that it was because they were not of his sheep that they did not believe in his message.

> "But ye believe not, because ye are not of my sheep, as I said unto you. My sheep hear my voice, and I know them, and they follow me."[126]

Therefore, Jesus in his own words gave us proof that the Jews were not of his sheep, the house of Israel. They were not Israelites. Jesus knew that they didn't have the same religion or ethnicity that he had.

Jacob kept his line pure and God rewarded him by making him the father of God's "chosen people."[127] Note that the Jews are not the "chosen people" even though they say that they are. Jacob's brother Esau married out of his own people and God punished him. His descendants moved to the Mount Seir area southeast of the Dead Sea. His descendants were called Edomites.[128] They were the ancestors of the people known today as Jews.[129] Later the Edomites moved into the areas vacated by the Israelites during the Captivity. Many years after that when John Hyrcanus, one of the Macabean kings, conquered the Edomites and then offered them full citizenship if they would adopt the religion then in place in Judea, this brought most of the Edomites into Judea and into the religion later known as Judaism.

> "As far as authentic history will carry us, the descendants of the Edomites are to be sought for rather amongst the Jews themselves, than amongst any other people ...."[130]

The Edomite Jews claimed they were from Abraham, which they were, being descended from Esau, a son of Isaac. But a passage in John proves that the Jews were not Israelites since they told Jesus that they had never been in bondage.[131] Of course, the Israelites had been held as slaves in Egypt.[132] Those were Edomite Jews to whom Jesus was speaking.

The Jews at the time of Jesus were not a part of any tribe of Israel, including the Tribe of Judah. They were a mixture of Babylonians, Cannanites, Hittites, but mainly Edomites. The Jews of today are the descendants of those people.[133] Jesus was not a Jew but was actually an Israelite, as he was descended from Levi through Aaron and Zadok.[134] He was also an Israelite because he was descended from Judah through David.[135] Both Levi and Judah were sons of Jacob who was renamed Israel by God. During his ministry Jesus had many battles with the Pharisees who were Edomite Jews, and not Israelites.[136] The Pharisees were not respected by Jesus because they enforced the Tradition of the Elders, later known as Judaism, which Jesus did not accept.[137] Also, Jesus did not respect them because he knew that they were Edomite Jews and not Israelites.

Jesus was of the religion of Hebrewism; or, as we call it today, the Religion of the Old Testament, and he was an Israelite of the Tribes of Levi and Judah. So, contrary to what is said or written about Jesus being a Jew, he was not a Jew either by religion or by ethnicity, including ancestry.[138]

RHN
AND
ELN

40

Section 3
A Genealogical Chart Showing a Descent Line From Joseph of Arimathea into Modern Times

Researched by Robert H. Nelson and Emma L. Nelson

Matthat

Heli (Eliakim/Joachim)
Miriam (**Mary**)
Yeshua (**Jesus**)

Joseph of Arimathea

Bianca
Elizabeth
John the Baptist

Anna
Penarddun
Bran
Caradoc
Cyllin
Ystradwl
Althildis
Clodimir IV
Farabert
Sunno
Hilderic
Bartherus
Clodius III
Walter
Dagobert I
Genebald
Dagobert II
Clodius
Marcomir
Pharamond
Clodius
Sigimerus
Ferreolus
Ausbert
Arnoldus
Dode Clothilde
Anchises
Pippin
Charles Martel
Pippin

Charlemagne

Pippin
Bernard
Pippin
Herbert I
Herbert II
Albert I
Herbert III
Otho
Herbert IV
Adelaide de Vermandois

Isabel de Vermandois

Ada de Warenne
William I, The Lion, King of Scotland
Isabel of Scotland
William de Ros
William de Ros
Lucy de Ros
William de Plumpton
Alice de Plumpton
Margaret de Sherburne
Richard (de Bayley) de Sherburne
Richard Sherburne
Agnes Sherburne
Nicholas Rushton
Agnes Rushton
Peter Worthington
Isabel Worthington
Peter Worden
Eleanor Worden
John Adams
Sarah Adams
Susannah Cowperthwaite
Grace Webster
Hugh Shotwell
John Shotwell
Catherine Shotwell
John Shotwell Goe
Dorcas Rebecca Colvin Goe

The genealogical descent lines shown here illustrate the more recent ancestors of Dorcas Rebecca Colvin Goe (1849-1929) and John Heaton Gans (1849-1927) who both descended from Joseph of Arimathea and who married each other, combining their ancestors for succeeding generations.

The earlier line to Isabel de Vermandois separates into the lines of two of her children: Ada de Warenne, her daughter with her second husband, William de Warenne, 2nd Earl of Surrey, and Robert de Beaumont, her son with her first husband, Robert de Beaumont, 1st Earl of Leicester.

Robert de Beaumont
Robert de Beaumont
Margaret de Beaumont
Roger de Quincy
Elena de Quincy
Roger la Zouche
Alan la Zouche
Maud la Zouche
Maud de Holland
Robert de Swynnerton
Maud de Swynnerton
Margaret Savage
Eleanor Dutton
Janet Langford
Alice Thelwall
John ap Harri Wynne
Rhys ap John Wynne
John ap Rhys Wynne
Thomas ap John Wynne
Dr. Thomas Wynne
Sydney Wynne
Anne Chew   Margaret Chew
Susannah Randall------Benjamin Brown
Richard Brown
Martha Patty Brown
Alpheus Gans
John Heaton Gans

Bertha Happy Gans
1879-1968

The Menorah was originally the function
and symbol of the Israelite priesthood, but it
was usurped by Edomite Jews and Judaism.

Part Two

The Priestly Ancestry

"And now, my children, I warn you,
fear the Lord your God with all your heart,
and walk plainly in all things according to his law."[1]

Levi

Section 4
The Priestly Ancestry

The priestly ancestry of Joseph of Arimathea and Jesus has been a topic of speculation since the time that they were both living. Biblical scholars point to the family connection that Jesus had to John the Baptist since, as cousins of some sort, they felt that there must also be a connection to the priestly descent line for Jesus.[2] Even though John the Baptist was known to be descended from Levi through Aaron by way of his mother Elizabeth and his father Zacharias, it has always been unclear how John the Baptist's connection to the priestly descent line pertains to Joseph of Arimathea and Jesus.

We will definitively show with an explanation below (and in a chart in Section 6 of this book) how Joseph of Arimathea and Jesus were connected to the priestly descent line, and how they both descended from Levi through Aaron, and accordingly from Zadok, and Simon the Just.[3]

The priestly descent line of Joseph of Arimathea and Jesus (beginning with Levi and then through his great-grandson, Aaron) is traced through the early High Priests prior to connecting with a non-royal descent line from King David, through his son Nathan, as shown in Luke.[4] That descent line, which included most of the High Priests, then continues on through Joseph of Arimathea, the great-uncle of Jesus, on through the ancestors of Charlemagne, and then on into modern times.

That priestly line is the same line that made Jesus and his brothers eligible to be High Priests, contrary to the incorrect statement in the Epistle to the Hebrews[5] that Jesus was not of the priestly line from Aaron. (See the details later in this section.) His half-brother James ultimately performed the High Priest functions with the Jerusalem Nazarene synagogue until his death in A.D. 62. Simeon, another half-brother of Jesus, followed James as the leader of the Jerusalem Nazarene synagogue,[6] and also performed the High Priest functions that are carried out only by direct descendants of Aaron. God's commands regarding his priestly line are shown here:

> "And take thou unto thee Aaron thy brother, and his sons with him … that he may minister unto me in the priest's office, even Aaron, Nadab and Abihu, Eleazar and Ithamar, Aaron's sons."[7] "It shall be a statute for ever unto him and his seed after him."[8]

The descent line of Joseph of Arimathea and Jesus from Aaron included most of the High Priests of ancient Judah and Israel.

Aaron

Aaron was the older brother of Moses and the first High Priest of Israel. He was, therefore, the progenitor of the Aaronic line of High Priests, which passed in a hereditary manner from father to son. (See the detailed statement about Aaron in Section 5 of this book.)

Eleazar

Eleazar succeeded his father, Aaron, as High Priest during the wanderings in the wilderness following the exodus from Egypt. He was the third of four sons of Aaron and his wife Elisheba. He and his brothers were anointed to serve as priests on the day that the Tabernacle was consecrated. However, Eleazar's two older brothers, Nadab and Abihu, were consumed by fire soon after that because they used incorrect fire at the altar.[9] After their deaths, Eleazar and his younger brother Ithamar, were in charge of the duties of the sanctuary and continued to perform the rituals for many years. That included the overseeing of the movement of the sanctuary from camp to camp as they moved through the wilderness. Much later, in a ceremony on Mount Hor when Aaron was close to death, Moses took the sacred vestments from Aaron and placed them on Eleazar.[10] At that time Eleazar succeeded to the office of High Priest. He held that office for over twenty years. Neither Moses nor Aaron lived to enter the Promised Land, but Eleazar did. As High Priest he assisted in the distribution of the land after the conquest.

Phineas

Phineas succeeded his father Eleazar as High Priest. He was renowned for his stand against the immorality which was then rampant among the Israelites. At that time the Moabites and Midianites had successfully lured Israelite men into idolatrous practices because of their associations with non-Israelite women.[11] As a result God had sent a plague to punish them. Phineas is recognized as the one who fought against those idolatrous practices, "so the plague was stayed from the children of Israel."[12]

Abishuah

Abishuah followed his father Phineas as High Priest. He was a great-grandson of Aaron and the fourth High Priest of the Israelites.[13]

Bukki

Bukki succeeded his father Abishuah as High Priest. He was the fifth High Priest of the Israelites, and the great-great-grandson of Aaron.[14]

This image shows an early High Priest performing his functions.[15]

Uzzi

Uzzi followed his father Bukki as High Priest.[16] A civil war broke out during High Priest Uzzi's years of service. As a result, there was a division among the people. Some followed Uzzi and others followed Eli. Eli was descended from Ithamar, a brother of Eleazar, and for several generations the office of High Priest left the line of Eleazar.

The next four descendants in the patrilineal line from Aaron through Eleazar did not serve as High Priest:

Zerahiah

Merioth

Amariah

Ahitub

Zadok

Zadok was in the direct patrilineal descent line from Eleazar, the son of Aaron.[17] The position of High Priest returned to the line of Eleazar when Zadok became a High Priest during the reign of King David. Zadok and Abiathar, a descendant of Ithamar, served together as High Priests during King David's reign.[18] They were both active in support of King David during his battle to put down the revolt of his son Absolom. Much later, when David was close to death, another of his sons, Adonijah, tried to take over the throne. The High Priest Abiathar supported Adonijah in that effort. Zadok remained loyal to King David and, in fact, assisted in the anointing of Solomon, David's chosen son to succeed him. Zadok then became the only High Priest. Later, he officiated at the dedication of Solomon's Temple and became the first High Priest to serve in Solomon's Temple, serving for a major part of Solomon's reign.[19]

Ahimaaz

Ahimaaz, the son of Zadok, was the next High Priest.[20] As his father had, Ahimaaz remained loyal to King David during his battle with Absolom. Ahimaaz is credited with conveying intelligence to David concerning Absolom's plans, and it was Ahimaaz who first reported the defeat of Absolom's forces. Ahimaaz served as High Priest during the latter part of King Solomon's reign.

Azariah

Azariah succeeded his father Ahimaaz as High Priest,[21] and also served at King Solomon's Temple. He was High Priest during the reign of Rehoboam.

The next seven descendants in the patrilineal line from Aaron through Eleazar did not serve as High Priest:

Johanan

Azariah

Amariah

Ahitub

Merioth

Zadok

Azariah (Shallum)[22]

Hilkiah

The office of High Priest returned to Eleazar's line when Hilkiah became the High Priest during the reign of King Josiah. The people of Judah had strayed from the teachings of God and had become idolatrous people. Although God's word remained in the memories of many, the Book of the Law had disappeared, and the Laws were not being followed. High Priest Hilkiah is credited with finding the lost copy of the Book of the Law in the Temple at Jerusalem during the time when the Temple was being renovated at the direction of King Josiah.[23] Also, it was he who oversaw the destruction of all of the symbols of idolatry and the return to obedience to God's laws.

Azariah IV

Azariah IV succeeded his father Hilkiah as High Priest.[24] He served during the last years of Solomon's Temple before Nebuchadnezzar destroyed it in 587 B.C.

Seraiah

Seraiah succeeded his father Azariah IV as High Priest,[25] and was the last High Priest before the Babylonian Captivity. He was killed by the king of Babylon, Nebuchadnezzar.[26]

Josedech

Josedech was the son of Seraiah[27] and was carried as a captive to Babylon, where he died. He did not serve as High Priest.

Joshuah

When the Israelites returned after the Captivity in Babylon, Joshuah (c. 515-490 B.C.), the son of Josedech and grandson of Seraiah, became the next High Priest. He assisted in the planning of the reconstruction, and the actual rebuilding, of the Temple.[28]

Joachim

Joachim (c. 490-470 B.C.) succeeded his father, Joshuah, as High Priest and assisted in the rebuilding of the Temple.[29]

Eliashib

Eliashib (c. 470-433 B.C.) succeeded his father, Joachim, as High Priest.[30] He rebuilt part of the wall of Jerusalem. He also scandalously provided rooms within the second Temple for the family of his wife, an Ammonite.[31]

Jeiadah

Jeiadah (c. 433-410 B.C.), son of Eliashib,[32] was High Priest during the reigns of Athaliah and Joash. He was married to Princess Jehoshiba who was the daughter of King Jehoram and the sister of King Ahaziah. King Ahaziah died soon after Jeiadah and Jehoshiba were married, and King Ahaziah's widow, Queen Athaliah, killed the members of King Ahaziah's family in order to take over the throne herself. Jeiadah and Jehoshiba were able to save the youngest of the royal children, the baby Joash, from being killed. They hid him, the only surviving heir, in the Temple for about six years. Jeiadah then successfully staged a coup which resulted in Queen Athaliah being dethroned and killed.[33] High Priest Jeiadah is credited with renouncing Baal worship and working with King Joash to repair the second Temple which had been neglected during previous years.

Johanan

Johanan (c. 410-371 B.C.), son of Jeiadah,[34] succeeded his father as High Priest.

Juddual

Juddual (c. 371-320 B.C.) was High Priest after his father Johanan.[35] He served during the reign of Alexander the Great.

Onias

Onias (c. 320-280 B.C.) succeeded his father Juddual as High Priest.[36]

Simon the Just

Simon the Just (c. 280-260 B.C.) was the next High Priest, succeeding his father Onias.[37] He is considered to have been one of the greatest of the High Priests. He believed that "on three things the world rests: on the Law, on Divine Service, and on good works."[38] "He is celebrated for his justice, and for having repaired the temple of Jerusalem, which had fallen to decay, and surrounding the city with a wall."[39] Simon's daughter, whose name is unknown, married Mattathias (also known as Tobiah[40] or Tobias[41]) who was of the non-royal descent line of David through David's son Nathan. The line from the daughter of Simon the Just and Mattathias came down through Joseph, Janna, Melchi, Levi, and Matthat. Matthat was the father of both Joseph of Arimathea and Heli. Heli was the father of Mary and the grandfather of Jesus.[42]

The following information refutes a belief of early Christian church fathers, and even current Christian apologists, the belief being that Jesus was not of the Levitic priestly line. That belief is false, and it is incorrectly stated in the Epistle to the Hebrews, which was attributed to Paul in the King James Version of the Bible, but now is thought not to have been written by him. It was possibly written by Priscilla, a follower of Paul, a few years before the destruction of Jerusalem which occurred in A.D. 70. In the Epistle to the Hebrews it is clearly, but erroneously, stated that Jesus was only of the line of Judah and not of the priestly line of Levi through Aaron.

> "For it is evident that our Lord sprang out of Juda; of which tribe Moses spake nothing concerning priesthood."[43]

This erroneous conclusion on the part of the writer of the Epistle to the Hebrews necessitated the concocting of the belief that Jesus was of a "superior" priestly line, that of Melchisedec.[44] That was another Christian myth and falsehood. There can not be a line that is superior to that established by God, "an everlasting priesthood throughout their generations."[45]

Furthermore, Jesus <u>was</u> descended from Levi through Aaron. (See Section 6.) That point is further supported by the fact that two of his half-brothers, James and Simeon, sons of Mary, the mother of Jesus, served as High Priests with the Jerusalem Nazarene synagogue which would have required descent directly from Aaron.

RHN
AND
ELN

Section 5
Aaron: The First High Priest of Israel

"The name of Aaron is connected with some of the most remarkable events in Sacred History. He is known to every reader of the Bible as the first high-priest of the Hebrew nation, and the brother of its inspired law giver, Moses. He bore a principal part in carrying into effect the deliverance from Egyptian bondage which God wrought for the Israelites, and in establishing that system of religious polity by which they have ever since been distinguished from all the nations of the world."[46]

Aaron was a great grandson of Levi, one of the twelve sons of Jacob. Aaron's father was Amram, and his mother was Jochebed. Both parents were of the tribe of Levi. Aaron had an older sister named Miriam and a younger brother named Moses. All three were born during the time of the captivity of the Israelites in Egypt. Aaron was born before the Egyptian pharaoh ordered the killing of all male Israelite infants, but Moses was born three years later, after that edict. Because of the ploy of his mother and sister, Moses was saved from death and, amazingly, was raised in the palace as a son of the pharaoh's daughter.[47]

While their brother, Moses, was being raised and educated in the Egyptian court, Aaron and Miriam remained with their own family among the other Israelites who were all enslaved by the Egyptians. There, Aaron gained a reputation for eloquent and persuasive speech.[48] "When he was grown up, he married Elisheba, the daughter of Abinadab, a prince of the tribe of Judah, and he had four sons … Nadab and Abihu, Eleazer and Ithamar, as a result of this marriage."[49]

Much later, after Moses had become an adult, had fled Egypt, and had lived in the Midian Desert for many years, he was told by God that he would be the one to lead his people out of Egyptian slavery. He was directed to return to Egypt, and Aaron was sent by God to meet his brother in the desert and assist him.[50] God "had spoken to him in Egypt, saying: 'Go into the wilderness to meet Moses,' and so precise was he in following the instructions given him, that he arrived at the sacred mountain just at the time his brother arrived there. They were glad again to look upon each other, and affectionately embraced, when we may suppose they gave each other a relation of the events of their lives for the last forty years."[51]

Aaron helped Moses make contact with the Israelite elders since he was unknown after being away for so many years. Also, Aaron served as the spokesman for Moses since he was an eloquent speaker and Moses was not.[52] Together they confronted the Egyptian pharaoh. Aaron was eighty-three years old when he and Moses spoke to the pharaoh.[53] They demanded that their people be freed, but the pharaoh repeatedly refused. He was eventually convinced to free the Israelites, but only after numerous pleas and after God's power was revealed to him through a series of miracles and plagues which were carried out by Aaron and Moses. Having received the pharaoh's word that they could leave, the thousands of Israelites fled in a tremendous exodus from Egypt by way of the Red Sea which divided to enable them to cross on dry land. By then, the pharaoh had reconsidered and sent his armies in pursuit. The Egyptians attempted to follow the Israelites across the Red Sea, but they were all drowned when the waters returned to their normal position.[54]

During the many years that the Israelites wandered through the wilderness searching for the Promised Land, Aaron continued to provide important support to Moses. Also, when Moses was absent he resolved the problems among the people.

After the escape from Egypt, the Tribe of Levi was set aside for the priestly service. Moses received the instructions from God regarding the priesthood, including the very detailed directions concerning the tabernacle and the duties of the priests. The duties of the priests involved caring for the tabernacle and following the rituals meticulously. All of the fixtures were described in detail. For example, Aaron was instructed to maintain the lampstand, or Menorah, in the tabernacle. He was to "make a candlestick of pure gold: of beaten work shall the candlestick be made: his shaft and his branches, his bowls, his knops and his flowers, shall be of the same. And six branches shall come out of the sides of it; three branches … out of the one side, and three branches … out of the other side."[55]

Aaron was designated as the first High Priest,[56] and it was directed that all future High Priests would be direct descendants of Aaron.[57] The High Priest would be an inherited position, going from father to oldest son. Aaron and his sons were all anointed with holy oil by Moses, and Aaron was invested with the priestly robes and accessories. "While the ordinary Priest had on a garment closely fitting the body, a coat, a girdle, and a covering for the head, the High Priest had in addition a robe denoting his superiority, an Ephod, a breast-plate, and a plate of gold on his forehead. The robe was of blue, woven from the top to the bottom without seam, being fastened with a girdle and variously ornamented. The sacred Ephod, or Ephod of the High Priest, was variously colored and ornamented with gold, and had upon each of the shoulders a large button, in which was set a precious stone, and in the stones were engraved the names of the twelve tribes of Israel. It was composed as a garment of 'gold, blue, scarlet, and fine twined linen with cunning work.' The breast-plate which he wore was four square, 'a span shall be the length thereof, and a span the breadth thereof,' and fastened with rings to the sacred Ephod. There were twelve precious stones set in the plate, three in a row, and on each stone was engraved the name of a son of Jacob as the head of a tribe of Israel, so that Aaron bore upon his breast, as well as upon his shoulders, the names of the various tribes. Upon the forehead was placed the figured golden plate, on which was engraved the motto: 'Holiness to the Lord.' This has been called the grand badge of the sacred office, and the motto was certainly appropriate for one engaged as Aaron in a holy calling."[58]

Illustration of Consecration of Aaron[59]

There were those within the Levite tribe who questioned the Aaronic priesthood and wished to set up a system of sacrifice of their own. They were condemned by God and disappeared into an opening in the earth.[60] All discontent was settled further when Moses took twelve rods, one from each of the tribes, and wrote the name of each tribe on its rod. On the rod for the tribe of Levi Moses wrote Aaron's name. Then he placed the rods near the sanctuary. The following day when the rods were examined it was discovered that all of the rods remained unchanged except for Aaron's. His rod had budded and bloomed and produced almonds. That was viewed as evidence of Aaron's right to the office, and his authority was not questioned again.[61]

The Israelites wandered through the wilderness for forty years in search of the Promised Land. During almost all of that time Aaron performed the duties of High Priest. When Aaron was close to death he, his son Eleazar, and Moses journeyed to Mt. Hor. Moses removed Aaron's priestly vestments and placed them on Eleazar. Soon after that, Aaron died. The people of Israel mourned him for thirty days.[62] His grave was unmarked so that the Israelites would not be tempted to worship him because of his abundant virtues, rather than God. Aaron had performed "the duties of his office with honor to himself, glory to God, and acceptability to the people, until his mission was ended ...."[63]

RHN
AND
ELN

Section 6
A Genealogical Chart Showing a Descent Line
From Aaron to Joseph of Arimathea and Jesus
(connecting with a non-royal descent line from David, through Nathan)
Researched by Robert H. Nelson and Emma L. Nelson

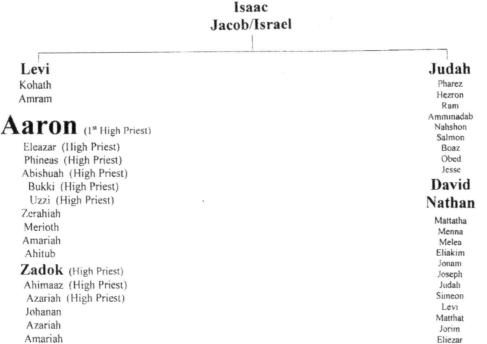

Abraham
Isaac
Jacob/Israel

Levi
Kohath
Amram

Aaron (1ˢᵗ High Priest)
Eleazar (High Priest)
Phineas (High Priest)
Abishuah (High Priest)
Bukki (High Priest)
Uzzi (High Priest)
Zerahiah
Merioth
Amariah
Ahitub
Zadok (High Priest)
Ahimaaz (High Priest)
Azariah (High Priest)
Johanan
Azariah
Amariah
Ahitub
Merioth
Zadok
Azariah (Shallum)
Hilkiah (High Priest)
Azariah IV (High Priest)
Seraiah (High Priest)
Josedech
Joshuah (High Priest)
Joachim (High Priest)
Eliashib (High Priest)
Jeiadah (High Priest)
Johanan (High Priest)
Juddual (High Priest)
Onias (High Priest)
Simon "The Just" (High Priest)
Daughter of Simon "The Just" -

Judah
Pharez
Hezron
Ram
Amminadab
Nahshon
Salmon
Boaz
Obed
Jesse
David
Nathan
Mattatha
Menna
Melea
Eliakim
Jonam
Joseph
Judah
Simeon
Levi
Matthat
Jorim
Eliezar
Joshua
Er
Elmadam
Cosam
Addi
Melchi
Neri
Shealtiel
Zerubbabel
Rhesa
Joanna
Joda
Joseph
Semein
Mattathias
Maath
Naggi
Esli
Nalium
Amos
Mattathias

Joseph
Janna
Melchi
Levi
Matthat

Heli (Eliakim/Joachim)   **Joseph of Arimathea**   Bianca
Miriam **(Mary)**   Elizabeth
                              Anna
Yeshua **(Jesus)**   Penarddun   **John the Baptist**

57

This image of a crown is part of a mosaic in Jerusalem which portrays the Twelve Tribes of Israel. The crown, which is included in the section depicting the Tribe of Judah, represents the royalty of the kingdom which was given to Judah.

Part Three

The Royal Ancestry

"For the Lord hath sworn to me,
that the kingdom of me, and of my seed, shall never fail ...."[1]

Judah

Section 7
The Royal Ancestry

The descent line of Joseph of Arimathea and Jesus, beginning with Judah, the son of Jacob, continues down to modern times. It went through the kings of Judah, including David, Solomon, Hezekiah, and Josiah. It was then traced through a granddaughter of King Josiah, Princess Tamar (the daughter of Crown Prince Johanan),[2] who married Neri who himself descended from King David through his son Nathan.[3] The line, from David through Solomon, Hezekiah, Josiah, and Princess Tamar then continued down to Jesus through his mother, and then on to the present time through the relatives of Jesus, including Joseph of Arimathea.

We will show in a chart on page 87, in Section 9, of this book how Joseph of Arimathea and Jesus are connected to the royal descent line of the kings of Judah, and how they both descend from Judah through David, and also from most of the other kings of Judah.

The descent line coming down to Joseph of Arimathea and Jesus included the following rulers of Judah:

David

King David, the greatest king of Judah and Israel, was born about three thousand years ago. He was a shepherd, a musician, a poet, a warrior, and a leader whose natural charisma inspired the loyalty and devotion of others. He endured many difficulties in his life and made serious mistakes, but he consistently demonstrated his faith in God and came to represent the epitome of the ideal ruler. (See the detailed statement about David in Section 8 of this book.)

Solomon

After the death of David, his son Solomon became king of Israel (which included Judah). Solomon reigned for forty years[4] (about 968-928 B.C.), and during that time his kingdom prospered, both materially and culturally. He built the Temple to house the Ark of the Covenant.[5] Numerous other enormous construction projects were completed, resulting in examples of architectural splendor, improved military fortifications, and enhanced infrastructure. Commerce flourished. Solomon's fame spread, and he was renowned for his wisdom. He wrote proverbs which are recorded in the Old Testament.[6] His vast realm exuded wealth and grandeur. His court included hundreds of wives and concubines, many of whom worshiped idols and did not follow God's laws. Solomon himself strayed from God's laws.[7]

Solomon Oversees the Construction of the Temple[8]

During Solomon's rule Israel reached great heights, but in achieving those successes he produced discontent among those who were heavily taxed and those who resented the preferential treatment given to the House of Judah. By the end of his reign the kingdom had started to collapse.

Rehoboam

When Solomon died Rehoboam became king. He was the son of Solomon and his wife Naamah, an Ammonite.[9] Rohoboam reigned for seventeen years[10] (about 928-911 B.C.), but he did not remain king of all of the Twelve Tribes of Israel. Soon after his reign began the ten northern tribes withdrew from the original kingdom that had been joined together under King David. They formed their own Kingdom of Israel with a capital in Samaria. That northern kingdom was eventually conquered by the Assyrians, and the descendants of those ten northern tribes became spread out and scattered, becoming what are still known as the Ten Lost Tribes of Israel. Only the tribes of Judah and Benjamin continued to be loyal to Solomon's successor. They inhabited the southern part of the former kingdom and had their capital in Jerusalem. The Kingdom of Judah was further weakened when it was invaded by Egyptian forces and became a vassal state of Egypt just a few years after Rehoboam became king.

Abijah

Abijah succeeded his father, Rehoboam, as king of Judah. Abijah's mother was Maacah, the granddaughter of Absolom.[11] Abijah was only king for about three years[12] (about 911-908 B.C.). During that time he battled against the armies of the Northern Kingdom of Israel in an unsuccessful attempt to reunite them with Judah.

Asa

Asa became king of Judah after his father Abijah. Asa reigned for forty-one years[13] (about 908-867 B.C.), and during those years he restored the strict adherence to Hebrewism. He rid the kingdom of idolatry and even had the queen mother, Maacah, deposed because of her involvement with foreign gods.[14] When the kingdom of Judah was in danger of being overwhelmed by the armies of Israel Asa was able to resist the attacks by forming an alliance with the king of Syria.

Jehoshaphat

Jehoshaphat succeeded his father as king of Judah about 867 B.C., and then continued to reign until about 851 B.C. Jehoshaphat was the son of Asa and his wife Azubah.[15] During his reign he created alliances with several different kings of Israel, and he "sought to the Lord God of his father, and walked in his commandments … and he had riches and honour in abundance."[16]

Jehoram

Jehoram followed his father Jehoshaphat as king of Judah and ruled for eight years[17] (about 851-843 B.C.). King Jehoram was married to Athaliah, the daughter of Ahab, the idolatrous king of Israel. They had a son Ahaziah, who was crown prince, and a daughter Jehosheba, who married the High Priest, Jeiadah.[18] Soon after his father's death Jehoram had his six brothers put to death.[19] King Jehoram "walked in the way of the kings of Israel, as did the house of Ahab: for the daughter of Ahab was his wife: and he did evil in the sight of the Lord."[20] Jehoram was very sick for the last two years of his life.

Ahaziah

Ahaziah, who is also called Jehoahaz, reigned for just one year[21] after his father's death in about 843 B.C. Ahaziah was killed by King Jehu of Israel. After his death, his mother, Athaliah, attempted to kill all of the royal descendants in order to secure her position as ruler of Judah. However, Jehosheba, the sister of Ahaziah, and wife of the High Priest, saved her youngest nephew, Joash, from being killed. She hid him and his nurse in the Temple for six years.[22]

Joash

Joash, the son of Ahaziah and Zibiah,[23] was kept safe within the Temple as a young child. When he was seven years old, the High Priest Jeiadah arranged that he be crowned and anointed king. Queen Athaliah was taken by surprise, led out of the Temple, and killed.[24] All of the altars to Baal were destroyed, and there was a general return to the worship of God. The observance of the Law continued until the High Priest Jeiadah's death.[25] Then Joash began to support the worship of other gods. Joash reigned from about 836 to 799 B.C. Towards the end of his life the kingdom of Judah was under attack from various enemies. Joash, himself, was severely wounded in battle, but his life actually ended when he was killed by his own servants.[26]

Amaziah

Amaziah, the son of Joash and his wife Jehoadden,[27] succeeded his father as king of Judah. When he became king he killed the men who had slain his father.[28]

During his reign (about 799-786 B.C.) he "did that which was right in the sight of the Lord, but not with a perfect heart."[29] He led his army into battle against the Edomites and had a decisive victory, but he began to worship some of the idols he had captured from the Edomites. Later he was defeated by the army of King Joash of Israel. That defeat resulted in his capture and hostages being taken, the destruction of parts of Jerusalem, and looting of the Temple and palace. That humiliating defeat was followed by Amaziah's death at the hands of his own men.[30]

Uzziah

Uzziah, the son of Amaziah and his wife Jecoliah, succeeded his father as king of Judah when he was just sixteen years old.[31] During his long period of power (about 786-758 B.C.) the Kingdom of Judah was very prosperous. Uzziah built fortifications and made agricultural improvements. He had a large fighting force that was well armed. He had weapons made that would sling arrows and stones from the towers, and his armies were victorious against their enemies.[32] During most of his reign he "did that which was right in the sight of the Lord ...."[33] But he arrogantly took it upon himself to burn incense upon the altar. The priests confronted him and "said unto him, It appertaineth not unto thee, Uzziah, to burn incense unto the Lord, but to the priests the sons of Aaron, that are consecrated to burn incense ...."[34] As Uzziah was at the altar he was struck with leprosy. He was no longer able to rule, and he lived separated from the others until his death.

Jotham

Jotham was the son of Uzziah and his wife Jerushah, who is sometimes known as Yerusha. "His mother's name also was Jerushah, the daughter of Zadok."[35] Jerushah was the daughter of Zadok (II) and she was in the direct line from Levi through Aaron and Eleazar. All of Jotham's descendants are, therefore, from Aaron through Eleazar as well as from David through Solomon, and thus they would all have both a priestly and a royal ancestral line. Jotham took charge after his father became a leper. His official reign began when he was twenty-five years old, after his father's death. He reigned alone for sixteen years from about 758 to 742 B.C.[36] The Kingdom of Judah continued to prosper under his leadership, and "Jotham became mighty, because he prepared his ways before the Lord his God."[37]

Ahaz

Ahaz succeeded his father as king of Judah when he was twenty years old and reigned for sixteen years (about 742-726 B.C.). He did not follow the good example set by his father, Jotham. Instead, he imitated the ways of the kings of Israel, building altars to the gods of the heathens and making human sacrifices.[38] He was embroiled in battles with the armies of Syria and northern Israel, and sought the protection of Assyria. Eventually, northern Israel was overwhelmed by Assyria and completely made a part of the Assyrian Empire. On the other hand the kingdom of Judah paid tribute to the Assyrians, and Ahaz was even further corrupted by them. He made many changes to the religious rituals and the Temple itself "for the king of Assyria."[39]

Hezekiah

Hezekiah succeeded his father Ahaz as king of Judah. He began to reign when he was twenty-five years old and ruled for twenty-nine years (about 726-697 B.C.). His mother was Abijah,[40] and his wife was Hephzibah.[41] Whereas Ahaz is recognized for the evil that he did in turning away from the traditions of the Temple, Hezekiah is renowned for his goodness. Almost immediately after assuming control of the kingdom he began to enact religious reforms that served to undo the harm his father had caused. He rallied the Levites to sanctify themselves and the Temple. The Temple was purified and the rituals were restored. It was during Hezekiah's reign that the northern kingdoms of Israel were destroyed by the Assyrians. When the kingdom of Judah was threatened by the king of Assyria Hezekiah strengthened his fortifications and trusted in God's deliverance. The kingdom of Judah and Hezekiah prospered greatly. He was highly regarded, and when he died he was buried in the "chiefest of the sepulchres of the sons of David: and all Judah and the inhabitants of Jerusalem did him honour at his death."[42]

Manasseh

Manasseh, the only son of Hezekiah and Hephzibah, began ruling when he was twelve years old. He reigned for fifty-five years[43] (about 697-642 B.C.), longer than any other king of Judah. Soon after becoming king he reversed the many religious reforms his father had enacted and emulated the wickedness of his grandfather, Ahaz. "No evil practice of the heathen … was too evil for his imitation; no superstition too grovelling for him to abase himself to its level."[44] He was the first king following the destruction of the kingdom of Israel and the dispersion of its people to other lands, and so he was not involved in waging war with Israel, as had many of the previous kings of Judah. Manasseh himself was captured, imprisoned, and eventually released by the king of Assyria, with whom he then allied himself. He was king of Judah for thirty-two more years after his release. During that time he tried to undo the evil practices of his earlier reign and lead his people back to the correct worship of God, but was not able to completely accomplish that.

Amon

Amon, the son of Manasseh and Meshullemeth,[45] succeeded his father as king of Judah when he was twenty-two years old. "He did that which was evil in the sight of the Lord … for Amon sacrificed unto all the carved images which Manasseh his father had made, and served them, and humbled not himself before the Lord, as Manasseh his father had humbled himself; but Amon trespassed more and more."[46] Amon was killed by his servants[47] after reigning in Jerusalem for only two years (about 642-641 B.C.).

Josiah was a king of Judah (641-609 B.C.) who instituted major reforms.[48]

Josiah

Josiah was the son of Amon and Jedidah. He was only eight years old when he became king after his father's assassination. He ruled for thirty-one years (about 641-609 B.C.).[49] "While he was yet young he began to seek after the God of David his father …."[50] He ordered that the Temple be repaired and renovated. During his grandfather's reign it had been adapted for worship of idols. During the process of restoring the Temple the High Priest Hilkiah found a scroll which was described as the Book of the Law. The scroll was taken to King Josiah and read. It detailed the calamities that were going to befall Judah because of her disobedience to God's laws over the years. It was verified by a prophetess that the evils that were described would occur, but not until after King Josiah's death. Desiring to avert the threatened judgments, he assembled all of the elders and read to them from the book of the Mosaic Law. They all entered into a covenant, agreeing to observe all of the statutes.[51] "The ark was restored to its proper place, the temple was purified, idolatrous utensils were removed, and those appropriate to the worship of God substituted in their room. After these preparations, the passover was observed with singular zeal and magnificence."[52] Josiah purged all of Judah of idolatry and returned the kingdom to strict compliance to God's laws.[53] For most of Josiah's reign there was peace. However, Josiah was killed by wounds inflicted during a battle to block the advance of Egyptian forces. "All Judah and Jerusalem mourned for Josiah. And Jeremiah lamented for Josiah …."[54]

Another interesting and renowned ancestor of Joseph of Arimathea and Jesus was discovered in the course of our research on the kings of Judah, the prophet Isaiah. Hephzibah, the mother of Manasseh, and the wife of King Hezekiah,[55] was the daughter of Isaiah the Prophet. The evil Manasseh had his grandfather, Isaiah the Prophet, "apprehended, and put … to death, by sawing him in two with a wooden saw."[56]

Isaiah was the son of Amoz, and he was in the line from the kings of Judah. He descended from David through Solomon and through Joash. (See the chart on page 87, in Section 9, for information showing some ancestors and descendants of Isaiah the Prophet.)

We are reminded that when Jesus returned to his hometown he would read in the local synagogue from the Torah and the Prophets, including, presumably, those passages written by his direct ancestor Isaiah. The reading of Jesus recorded in the Gospel of Luke[57] was from Isaiah 61[58] which was actually written by a later, unknown prophet, and not by his famous ancestor.[59]

RHN
AND
ELN

Section 8
King David: His Life and His Eternal Throne

King David is one of the most illustrious and well-known figures in all of history, with abundant details of his life having been documented in the Bible. His name is mentioned more often than any other in the Bible. Stories about David are contained in various parts of the Old Testament, most notably in the two books of Samuel, the first book of Kings, and the first book of Chronicles. Seventy-three Psalms are attributed to David, and there are numerous references to him in the New Testament. He is renowned as a ruler, a warrior, a poet, and a musician. David, king of Judah and Israel, was the originator of the prestigious Davidic Bloodline.

David was born in Bethlehem about three thousand years ago. He was the youngest son of Jesse, whose lineage traced back to Abraham.[60] Abraham, a Hebrew, is recognized as the first of his people to reject polytheism and accept the concept of one God. Abraham's son Isaac was the father of Jacob, whose name was changed to Israel. Jacob had twelve sons, Israelites, from whom the twelve separate tribes of Israel arose. One of those sons was Judah. Judah had twin sons, Pharez and Zerah, and it was from Pharez that David was descended.

Abraham and his family left Mesopotamia and inhabited Canaan, but widespread famine later forced his descendants to migrate into Egypt. At first they lived peacefully in Egypt, but eventually they were forced into slavery. The Old Testament book of Exodus tells of their escape. Moses led the Israelites out of Egypt and they wandered for forty years. During that time Moses received the Ten Commandments which delineated a code of conduct which should be followed, and they entered into a Covenant with God. Moses' older brother Aaron was his spokesman and became the first High Priest of the Israelites. Both Moses and Aaron died during the years of wandering, and Joshua led the Israelites into their promised land where they defeated those already living there. The Israelite tribes at that time lived as independent groups without a centralized government, but a military and religious leader called a judge would lead the combined tribes in times of crisis. Samuel the prophet was such a religious leader. After many years, though, the continual threats from others in the area, especially from the Philistines, created a need for them to more formally organize themselves and join together under one strong military leader and ruler. Samuel ordained Saul, a member of the tribe of Benjamin, as the first king of the Israelites, in 1049 B.C. King Saul was successful in leading the Israelites to victory in battles against the Philistines and various other antagonists. However, Saul failed to obey God's instructions, as delivered to him by Samuel, and so the royal line of succession was not passed on to his son.[61]

Samuel was told by God that the individual that would succeed Saul as king would be a son of Jesse who lived in Bethlehem. He arranged a meeting with Jesse and was introduced to seven of his eight sons, but realized that none of them was the chosen one. Samuel asked Jesse if he had any more sons, and Jesse told him that his youngest son was not there, but was tending the sheep. Then he summoned his youngest son, David, and presented him to Samuel. Recognizing that David was the future king that God intended, Samuel anointed him with oil, and so it was determined that the second king of Israel would be from the tribe of Judah.[62]

David was a shepherd. While still a boy he was responsible for caring for his father's flock of sheep. The time he spent tending his sheep would have provided the opportunity for him to develop characteristics for which he later became famous. Courage and strength were needed to defend the sheep from predators. It is said that David fought off both a bear and a lion by himself in order to protect his flock.[63] A shepherd spent long periods of time alone. This required self-reliance. This solitude also provided time that could be spent in meditation and in pursuing solitary interests and developing personal skills. Later in his life David was well-known for his poetry and his playing of the harp. "It was an appropriate training-place for the future king and bard of Israel, and no occupation could have been more conducive to the development in him of those qualities of prudence, promptitude, and prowess which his after-life required, than that of a shepherd."[64]

As a young man David was called to the court of King Saul because of his reputation as a musician. Saul wanted a harpist who could play music to help relieve his tormented mind. David stayed near the king and played for him frequently.[65] While dwelling in the palace he formed a close friendship with Jonathan, Saul's son. Saul himself grew more and more appreciative of David, because of the calming effect of his musical talent and also because of the bravery he demonstrated.

The Israelite army was involved in repeated battles with the Philistines. During one such conflict which took place in the Valley of Elah, the Philistines had a giant named Goliath who challenged the Israelites to send forward someone to fight him. His taunting continued for many days, but the Israelites could find no one with enough courage to vie one-on-one with an armored warrior so large. It happened that Jesse sent David to carry food to his older brothers who were serving in Saul's army, and David heard Goliath's challenge. He determined that he would be the one to represent the Israelites against the giant. He requested permission from King Saul, and convinced him that since he had previously slaughtered both a lion and a bear by himself he was capable of defeating Goliath. Saul attempted to dress David in his own armor, but it was too cumbersome for the youth. David chose to face Goliath with no armor and armed only with his staff, his slingshot, and some stones.[66]

Goliath was astounded to see that such an unthreatening-looking opponent had taken up his challenge and he taunted him, but David responded that he would be victorious because God was with him. David slung his first stone, and it hit his foe in the forehead. Goliath tumbled to the ground, and David rushed forward and used the giant's own sword to behead him. When the Philistines saw that their champion had been defeated they fled, and the Israelites pursued them and triumphed over them.[67]

David, After Having Killed Goliath[68]

71

David's victory over Goliath brought him immediate fame. It also resulted in his being given a military command by King Saul. Eventually he rose in rank to become second in command, under Abner, the head of the army. David's continued successes further increased his popularity, both with the general population and within the royal palace. Jonathan and David's friendship grew even stronger, and Michal, the king's daughter, fell in love with him. The fame and admiration he received made Saul extremely jealous and fearful of David. His ill-feelings turned to hate, and he made repeated attempts to kill David both directly and through various plots in which he placed David in situations in which he thought his death would result. Michal, who had become David's wife, helped him escape one of her father's plans to kill him,[69] and Jonathan warned him about another plot.[70] Finally, the danger to David's life became so imminent that he was forced to flee rapidly, unarmed and without food.

David first sought help at Nob, the city of priests. There he did not reveal that he was being pursued by Saul. When Ahemelech the priest questioned why he was alone, David became frightened and made up a fictitious story to explain his solitary condition. He asked for bread and a weapon. The priest gave him bread from the consecrated table and Goliath's sword which was kept there.[71] Then David continued his flight. When Saul later discovered that the priests had assisted David in his escape, though unknowingly, he ordered that all of the priests and others in the city of Nob be killed.[72]

After David left Nob he entered the land of the Philistines, seeking refuge with Achise the king of Gath. The servants of the king recognized that he was David who had slain Goliath, and they warned Achise. When David realized that he was in danger, he feigned madness. His deception was successful, and he was able to leave unharmed.[73]

David settled for a while in a cave of Adullum in the wilderness. He was joined there by his parents, other family members, and a growing band of followers. One of those who aligned himself with David was the priest Abiathar who was the sole survivor of the massacre at the sanctuary at Nob.[74] As his forces grew in number and strength David began to exert his military might while, at the same time, eluding Saul.

Learning that the city of Keilah was about to be attacked by the Philistines, David and his men fought against the Philistines and saved the city.[75] Saul heard about his presence in Keilah and assembled his armies to go to attack the city. David and his men, who numbered about six hundred at that time, left Keilah and fled once again from Saul and his army. They took refuge in the wilderness of Ziph to escape from him. Saul's son, Jonathan, sought David out in the woods, and consoled and encouraged him. The two friends made a covenant with each other, and then Jonathan returned to his home.[76]

Despite the fact that King Saul was searching for David and trying to kill him, David continued to respect Saul as God's anointed. He strove to evade Saul and not to harm him. On two occasions David had the opportunity to kill Saul, and both times he refused. One time Saul discovered that David was in the wilderness of En-gedi. He took three thousand of his men and went in pursuit of David. When Saul entered a cave to rest, David and his companions were hiding nearby. This was an excellent opportunity for David to kill Saul; but, instead, he cautioned his men not to harm Saul and he himself went into the cave and secretly cut off the bottom edges of his garment as he slept. Then, when Saul awoke and began to walk away, David called after him. He revealed to Saul how he had spared his life and that he had no intention of ever harming him.[77] Another time Saul pursued David in the wilderness of Ziph. When David learned that Saul and his troops had pitched their tents and were sleeping, he sneaked into their camp and located the spot where Saul was sleeping. David's companion wanted to kill Saul, but David stopped him. David then took Saul's sword and his jar of water without awakening anyone in the camp. When he was at a distance, he shouted to Abner the captain of Saul's army, and told him that he hadn't done a good job of protecting the king as he had been able to enter the camp and take Saul's sword. Saul heard David's voice and realized that once again David had spared him.[78]

When David was in the wilderness of Paran, he sought support from a wealthy man named Nabel, who had thousands of sheep and goats. He sent a small group of his men to inquire whether he would share some of the food that he had for his shearers with David and his men. Nabel rudely rebuffed the men. When they reported back to David he was furious and decided to take revenge against Nabel. He and his men approached Nabel's property, intending to kill him and all those in his household. Nabel's wife, Abigail, heard about what had happened, and she secretly went out with her servants bearing bread and wine and other foods for David and his men. When she met David and his forces she spoke eloquently to David, reminding him of God's great plans for him and pointing out that he would regret the rash killings. David was very appreciative that she interceded to prevent his impetuous plans from being carried out. It happened that about ten days after this all transpired Nabel died. Then David sent for Abigail, and she became one of his wives.[79]

David's existence as an exile in the wilderness continued for several years. Finally he again sought refuge with the Philistines. This time he was accepted by Achise of Gath, and David was given the town of Ziklag in which he and all of his men and their families could settle. It was a time of relative security for David. He was within the land of the Philistines and did not have to fear Saul, and he had the luxury of not having to continually move around through the wilderness. From their headquarters in Ziklag, David and his forces would ride out and attack various tribes that had been raiding towns in Judah. They would kill those enemies and return to Ziklag with the spoils of war: sheep, oxen, and camels. One of the tribes they attacked was the Amalekites.[80]

Eventually Achise requested that David and his men join his army in a battle against King Saul's forces. That presented a difficult dilemma for David, but he started out with his men following Achise and his Philistine army. Before reaching their destination, however, Achise was convinced by his men that it was too big of a risk to rely on David's fidelity when fighting against Israel. David and his men were asked to turn back. When they arrived back in Ziklag they found that while they had been gone their town had been plundered and burned by the Amalekites and their families had been captured. David and his men were distraught and overcome with grief, but then David asked Abiathar the priest to bring the ephod and he inquired of God and decided to try to overtake the enemy and recover their families that had been taken. They found an Egyptian servant who had been abandoned by his Amalekite master because he had fallen ill. They fed him and enlisted his help. From the information he provided they were able to locate the Amalekites and kill them. They succeeded in rescuing all of their families and recovering everything that had been taken. Also, they collected the flocks and herds of the enemy and additional spoils. David shared the spoils of war with all those who had followed him to Ziklag, and he also sent gifts of the spoils to the elders in Judah.[81]

Meanwhile, Achise and the Philistines had engaged the men of Israel in battle and had prevailed. Jonathan and two other sons of Saul were killed in the battle. Saul was seriously wounded by archers, and then fell on his own sword. It was a devastating defeat. Those of Israel who were not killed fled. The Philistines took over much of their land. When news of the battle reached Ziklag, David, and all of those with him, mourned the death of Saul and Jonathan and the others of the house of Israel.[82]

David was no longer a fugitive with a small band of followers. During his years of flight from Saul he had amassed a strong fighting force and allied himself with some powerful families in Judah.[83] After Saul's death he made his way back into Judah, succeeded in occupying it, and made Hebron in southern Judah his capital city. David ruled as king over the southern Kingdom of Judah for over seven years. During that time Saul's son Ishbaal, with the support of Saul's military leader Abner, reigned over the northern tribes of Israel. The two kingdoms waged war against each other. As their battles continued, David's strength gradually increased as Ishbaal's power waned.[84] Finally, after a quarrel between Abner and Ishbaal, Abner swung his support to David, and the war ended.

The pact between David and Abner was conditioned upon a promise from Ishbaal that his sister Michal would be returned to David. Michal, Saul's daughter, had married David before his escape to the wilderness. She did not accompany him when he fled, and her father gave her in marriage to another man during David's long enforced absence. Michal was reunited with David, as Ishbaal had agreed.[85] By the time that Michal returned to David he had six other wives and six sons.

Shortly after Abner decided to support David he was murdered by Joab, David's nephew. Joab killed Abner to avenge the death of his brother whom Abner had killed in battle. David was not a party to the killing of Abner, and greatly mourned his death.[86] Soon after that Ishbaal was also murdered, but by two captains of his own forces. The assassins went to David expecting his approval since Ishbaal had been fighting against David for so many years, but David admonished them for killing God's anointed and ordered that they both be executed.[87]

After the deaths of Abner and Ishbaal, elders from the tribes of Israel who had aligned themselves with Ishbaal came to David in Hebron and sought to become a part of his kingdom. In 1003 B.C. David became king of all Israel. He was thirty years old. One of the first things he did as king of the united kingdom of Judah and Israel was to move his capital city from Hebron. He moved northward and captured the city of Jerusalem from the Jebusites. Jerusalem, called Jebus at that time, was highly fortified. David and his men are believed to have been able to breach the defenses of the city by entering through passageways that carried water from the Gihon Spring. Jerusalem became the City of David and the capital of Israel. Hiram, the king of Tyre, sent skilled workmen and building materials to erect a palace for David in his new capital city.[88]

When the Philistines learned that David had become king of all Israel they waged war against his kingdom. David sought God's advice, as was his custom before taking up arms, and he felt confident that Israel would prevail. He had a well-organized army made up of very experienced, brave, and loyal warriors, commanded by Joab. His mighty fighting force was successful. The Philistines were vanquished and driven out of Israel. Although David had subdued the Philistines, conflicts with other neighboring nations continued for many years. David's forces were victorious, and his kingdom was greatly enlarged because of his victories. He also accumulated great wealth through the spoils of war and the tributes which were paid by the conquered nations.

King David recognized that Israel's security depended on God's blessing, and that obedience to God's laws was essential. Having established a secure place for his people, he knew that it was important then to have the Ark of the Covenant brought into Jerusalem. David gathered his people from all over Israel to accompany him, and they went together and got the Ark of the Covenant from its previous location in Baalah of Judah. It was a very festive occasion with the people singing and dancing and playing musical instruments as they moved along. The Ark was carried on a cart that was pulled by oxen, and at one point the oxen stumbled. Uzza, who was one of those driving the cart, reached out to keep the Ark from falling. When he touched the Ark he immediately fell over dead. David was very upset, for he realized then that they had displeased God by not following the proper procedure for moving the Ark. David decided to not bring the Ark the rest of the way to Jerusalem yet. Instead, he left it at the house of Obed-Edom for three months. During that time Obed-Edom and his family were greatly blessed, so David determined that it would now be safe to move the Ark again. This time David made sure that the proper rituals were being followed. He prepared a Tabernacle tent for it in Jerusalem. Then he assembled all of his people again, but told them that only the Levites could carry the Ark. The Levites sanctified themselves. The whole throng went as before, but the Levites assigned the proper musicians to sing and play the musical instruments. The Ark of the Covenant was retrieved from the house of Obed-Edom and carried on the shoulders of the Levites to the place that had been prepared for it in Jerusalem. David and thousands of others celebrated the movement of the Ark. David made burnt offerings to God and blessed his people. There was great rejoicing and dancing. David himself participated in praising God by dancing without restraint with his head and feet uncovered and wearing the priest's ephod. David returned to his household after the festivities, and was confronted by his wife Michal who had watched him dancing from her window and couldn't understand his complete elation. She castigated him for his undignified behavior. David responded by reminding her that God had chosen him, above her father, Saul, and all of her family, to be ruler over Israel.[89]

David had intended that the Tabernacle tent would be a temporary place to hold the Ark of the Covenant, and he hoped to build a Temple to be its more permanent home. He gathered materials and drew up plans for its construction. He told Nathan the Prophet about his plans. Nathan told him that God had revealed that David's house and throne would be established forever, but that he would not be the one who would build the Temple.[90]

Remembering his beloved friend Jonathan, David wondered whether there were any descendants of Saul to whom he could show kindness for Jonathan's sake. He asked Ziba, who had been one of Saul's servants. Ziba told him that Jonathan had a son Mephibosheth who was lame. Mephibosheth and his young son Micha were brought to the palace, and David restored to them the land that had been Saul's and instructed Ziba that he and his family should farm the land and be servants to Mephibosheth. Jonathan's son ate at the king's table from then on, with David's sons.[91]

After going to Jerusalem David had taken more concubines and had additional children. He also added another wife, Bathsheba, but the manner in which she became his wife is considered one of David's greatest sins. During one of Israel's conflicts David did not join his army in the battle, but remained in Jerusalem. One evening he was walking along the rooftop looking out over his city. From his vantage point he saw a beautiful woman bathing, and he inquired who she was. He was told that she was Bathsheba, the wife of Uriah the Hittite. Uriah was away fighting in the war. David sent for Bathsheba. Some weeks later she told him that she was pregnant. Realizing that it would be obvious that he had committed adultery, he tried to hide his sin. He had Uriah called back from the battle. When Uriah arrived at the palace David inquired about how the fighting was progressing. Then he sent him to his own house to be with his wife, but Uriah did not go to his house. Instead, he slept by the door of the palace where David's servants slept because he did not think that it was proper for him to have the luxury and comfort of being with his wife while his officers and fellow warriors were enduring the hardships of war. When that scheme did not work, David sent Uriah back to the battlefront, but he also sent a letter to Joab directing him to place Uriah in the most dangerous part of the fighting so that he would be among those who would die. Uriah was killed in battle, and when Bathsheba learned that her husband was dead she mourned for him. When the period of mourning was past David sent for Bathsheba, and she became his wife.[92]

After that, Nathan the Prophet went to David and rebuked him and revealed God's displeasure with how David had broken his commandments. David sought forgiveness for his sin, and Nathan told him that God would forgive him but also punish him. He told him that the sword would never depart from his house and that rebellion within David's own family would occur as punishment. He also revealed that the baby that Bathsheba had conceived would not live. The baby died several days after its birth.[93]

It was Absalom, David's third son, who rebelled against his father, as was prophesied. Absalom's mother was Maachal, the daughter of the king of Geshur. Absalom was handsome, charming, and ambitious; and he undermined his father's power. David's love for his son made him oblivious to Absalom's covert plotting. After quietly building support throughout Israel, Absalom orchestrated a well-organized revolt from his headquarters in Hebron. David was taken by surprise and forced to flee from Jerusalem with a small following. He went into the wilderness to organize his defense. Absalom did take over Jerusalem temporarily, but was ultimately unable to prevail against his father's army. Despite Absalom's strong following, once David had gathered his supporters and loyal allies, his forces were able to completely rout Absalom's men in just one battle. David was advised not to accompany his army to the engagement in order to ensure his safety. He complied, but ordered them to spare Absalom. That was not to be.

During the battle Absalom was caught by his hair in the branches of an oak tree, and killed by Joab and his armor bearers. When David was brought word of the successful defeat of the enemy, his first question was about the safety of Absalom. Hearing that his son had been killed he grieved greatly, and the day of victory was turned into a time of mourning.[94]

This is a photograph by Julia Margaret Cameron of Sir Henry Taylor who was portraying King David.[95]

As David grew older it was necessary for him to groom his successor. He had many sons who wanted to succeed him. Absalom had already unsuccessfully attempted to take over. Another son, Adonijah, was the son of Haggith. He was David's fourth son, and being the oldest son still living he assumed that he should be the heir apparent. Joab supported him in this ambition, and when David was frail and seemed about to die Adonijah proclaimed himself king.[96] Adonijah was not David's choice to be his successor.

Although David and his wife Bathsheba had a son who died soon after his birth, they also later had four more sons. The oldest of those sons was Solomon, and David had promised Bathsheba that Solomon would be king. Being aware of David's wishes, Bathsheba and Nathan the Prophet visited David as he lay oblivious in his bed. They told him that Adonijah was claiming the kingship, and reminded him that he had selected Solomon to succeed him. David's consciousness was stirred, and he directed them to carry Solomon on the king's mule to Gihon, and for Zadok the priest and Nathan the Prophet to anoint him king in front of the people. The instructions were followed and Solomon was proclaimed king in his father's stead, and the trumpets were blown and the people shouted, "God save the king." Adonijah heard the joyous commotion, and he and his followers accepted Solomon as king.[97]

Before his death David instructed Solomon about the responsibilities he would have. He reminded him about keeping God's statutes, and he also directed him to seek vengeance against David's enemies and to treat kindly those who had been loyal to him. He also transferred to Solomon all of the plans he had made for the construction of the Temple for the Ark of the Covenant. David died soon after he proclaimed Solomon the new king. He was about seventy years old and had been king for forty years, seven years ruling over Judah in Hebron and thirty-three years ruling over the combined tribes of Judah and Israel in Jerusalem.[98] He was buried in the City of David.

David had lived a long and momentous life. From a young shepherd boy he had been transformed into the most powerful ruler of his era and one of the most well-known figures of all time. The path he had to follow to get there was not an easy one. While just a young man he was identified as God's chosen one, and was anointed king by the prophet Samuel; but he had to wait many years and endure many hardships before he became king. He had to live as a fugitive for years as Saul pursued him relentlessly and tried to kill him.

"David was a skillful warrior, a talented musician, a loyal friend, and a gifted poet. Even when living in the wilderness as an outcast, his charisma and leadership qualities were evidenced by the large number of devoted followers who were attracted to his cause despite the dire circumstances. Once David became king he excelled as a ruler. He reunited the divided tribes of Israel and established Jerusalem as his capital. He developed Israel into the most powerful and highly regarded nation of that time. He expanded the territorial boundaries of his kingdom and accumulated great wealth for his realm. Although his empire was continually involved in conflicts with neighboring nations, David's armies were victorious. David was a giant of history, but he also made serious mistakes and committed sins for which he sought God's forgiveness. He attributed all that he achieved to God's blessings, and always remembered that he prevailed because God was with him."[99] His enduring trust in God is exemplified by his most famous poem, the 23rd Psalm:

> "The Lord is my shepherd; I shall not want. He maketh me to lie down in green pastures; He leadeth me beside the still waters. He restoreth my soul; He guideth me in straight paths for His name's sake. Yea, though I walk through the valley of the shadow of death, I will fear no evil, For Thou art with me; Thy rod and Thy staff, they comfort me. Thou preparest a table before me in the presence of mine enemies; Thou hast anointed my head with oil; my cup runneth over. Surely goodness and mercy shall follow me all the days of my life; And I shall dwell in the house of the Lord for ever."[100]

King David was promised by God that "thine house and thy kingdom shall be established for ever before thee: thy throne shall be established for ever."[101] The promise has been kept. For over four hundred years there was a King of Judah upon the Throne of David, ending in 587 B.C. when Zedekiah and all of his sons were captured and removed by Nebuchadnezzar. Since that time there has not been a king of Judah. However, the Throne of David, as prophesied, is ongoing and will last forever.

David's son Solomon succeeded him as king of Israel (which included Judah). He had a very long and exceedingly prosperous reign. His kingdom flourished during most of his reign, but King Solomon strayed from obedience to God's laws; and by the end of his reign his powerful, productive kingdom had begun to collapse. After the death of Solomon his son Rehoboam became king, but he did not remain king of the entire Twelve Tribes of Israel. Only the tribes of Judah and Benjamin continued to be loyal to Solomon's successor.

Kings of the royal line of David continued to rule through fifteen more monarchies, though they did not preside over kingdoms as large and prosperous as David and Solomon had led. During those years the Kingdom of Judah was often in a very unstable condition and at different periods was a vassal state to Assyria, Egypt, or Babylon. In 597 B.C. Zedekiah, a direct descendent of David, was installed as king by Nebuchadnezzar of Babylon. He would prove to be the last king of Judah.

During this era the prophet Jeremiah continually warned the inhabitants of the Kingdom of Judah that they must return to obeying the Covenant that had been made with God in order to avoid destruction. Jeremiah began his prophecies during the reign of King Josiah, around 625 B.C.

(Many people incorrectly believe that Jeremiah the Prophet was the grandfather of Zedekiah. The Jeremiah who was the grandfather of Zedekiah was from Libnah, and he had a daughter Hamutal who was a wife of King Josiah.[102] Jeremiah the Prophet was from Anathoth and was the son of Hilkiah who was a priest of Anathoth in the land of Benjamin.[103] Also, Jeremiah the Prophet was never married and had no descendants, and he stated that the "word of the Lord came also unto me, saying, Thou shalt not take thee a wife, neither shalt thou have sons or daughters in this place."[104])

Josiah was a pious king who enacted religious reforms to return his people to strict obedience to God's laws. He also ruled over the Kingdom of Judah during a period in which his country could govern itself without foreign interference. After Josiah's death in battle it was not long before his kingdom was no longer independent. During his sons' reigns the Egyptians and then the Babylonians took control, although the sons were still officially the rulers. The Kingdom of Judah reverted once again to idolatry and immorality. Jeremiah spoke courageously and repeatedly to the people of Jerusalem, warning them of the dangers that were imminent if they did not repent.

When Zedekiah, the last son of Josiah to become king, failed to heed his warnings and rebelled against Babylon, Jeremiah admonished him that God was sending Nebuchadnezzar to punish the Kingdom of Judah and that the only chance for survival was to submit to the Babylonians. Zedekiah still did not follow Jeremiah's advice, and imprisoned him instead. Then Zedekiah tried unsuccessfully to enlist the help of the Egyptians, and when that failed Nebuchadnezzar's army was able to besiege Jerusalem. The siege lasted about a year and a half. By then Jerusalem and its inhabitants were so weakened that the Babylonians were able to break through the walls of the city. Zedekiah tried to escape with his sons, but was captured. His sons were killed in front of him, and then he was blinded and imprisoned for the rest of his life. There would be no more kings of Judah.[105]

The city of Jerusalem, including the magnificent Temple that Solomon had built, was destroyed in 587 B.C. Many of the people of Jerusalem who were not killed were taken captive, but some of the poor people were allowed to remain and tend to the vineyards and fields. Nebuchadnezzar ordered his captain of the guard to free Jeremiah so that he could be among his people.

Jeremiah's prophecies had come to pass, but his work was not yet done. He had been enabled to speak God's words, but he was also commissioned to be an agent to bring about God's plan. Jeremiah stated:

> "Then the Lord put forth his hand, and touched my mouth. And the Lord said unto me, Behold, I have put my words in thy mouth. See, I have this day set thee over the nations and over the kingdoms, to root out, and to pull down, and to destroy, and to throw down, to build, and to plant."[106]

Jeremiah prophesied about and witnessed the destruction of his nation, but his role in building and planting was yet to reveal itself.

Baruch Writes Jeremiah's Prophecies (Jeremiah 36:4)[107]

During the capture of Jerusalem Jeremiah the Prophet had protected the daughters of Zedekiah, and also some precious historical relics from the Temple. After the invaders had left he remained near Jerusalem for a while consoling and encouraging the limited number of people who had survived. Nebuchadnezzar had installed Gedaliah as governor and placed him in charge of those who remained after the destruction of Jerusalem. Gedaliah resided in Mizpah, and it was there that Jeremiah and his people lived. Their numbers grew as others, realizing that a remnant of Judah remained in the care of the governor, returned to join them. However, the security that Gedaliah provided did not last for long. He and many of the people with him were killed by Ishmael and his forces. Others were carried away as captives. They were apprehended by Johanan, the son of Kareah, and his men, and the captives were released. Johanan urged all of the people to go to Egypt for safety. Jeremiah prophesied against going into Egypt, but his warnings were ignored and he, the king's daughters, and Baruch, his scribe, were taken forcibly into Egypt.[108] They remained there in Tahpanhes for a while, but then Jeremiah was warned by God that Nebuchadnezzar was about to invade Egypt. Realizing that it would no longer be safe there, he and a small group (including Baruch and one of Zedekiah's daughters, Princess Tephi) fled aboard a Phoenician ship. As it had been prophesied:

> "And the remnant that is escaped of the house of Judah shall again take root downward, and bear fruit upward: For out of Jerusalem shall go forth a remnant ...."[109]

They took with them the relics that Jeremiah had saved from the destruction of the Temple, including the harp of David, and the Stone of Destiny which was the stone pillow that Jacob had slept on as he dreamed of Jacob's ladder.[110]

Some scholars believe that the Ark of the Covenant was one of the relics that Jeremiah carried with him when he fled Egypt, but Jeremiah indicated that God did not think it was still important and it appears that Jeremiah did not feel any need to save it.[111]

(There are many theories that have been espoused over the centuries concerning the whereabouts of the Ark of the Covenant. One theory is that it is located in a desert site in Yemen known as Marib. Another idea is that it is hidden in the Temple Mount in Jerusalem. Some feel that it is in Egypt in the Great Pyramid of Giza. Another theory is that it is in the Church of Our Lady Mary of Zion in Axum, Ethiopia. Still another belief is that the Ark of the Covenant was brought back by Knights Templar during one of the crusades and then hidden in central England or in Lanquedoc, France. Another theory is that it was taken by Jeremiah to Tara in County Meath in Ireland.)

However, Jeremiah prophesied:

> "And it shall come to pass, when ye be multiplied and increased in the land, in those days, saith the Lord, they shall say no more, The ark of the covenant of the Lord: neither shall it come to mind: neither shall they remember it ...."[112]

Jeremiah and his companions traveled across the Mediterranean Sea, stopping in Gibraltar and Spain, and eventually they arrived in a bay off Cornwall at the southwest tip of what is now England. Then they sailed to their intended destination on the eastern side of what is now Ireland. They were met there by Oliolla who would become the husband of Princess Tephi.

Oliolla (also known as Eochaidh which means knight and Heremon which means high king) was a descendant of Judah, through Judah's son Zerah.[113, 114] Judah was the fourth son of Jacob and the founder of one of the Twelve Tribes of Israel, the Tribe of Judah.[115]

Jacob had blessed each of his sons, as he was about to die. Christians believe that his words in Genesis to Judah constitute a prophecy that the descent line from Judah will produce a messiah, or in Christian terms the Christ. In the King James Version of the Bible that passage is as follows:

> "The sceptre shall not depart from Judah, nor a lawgiver from between his feet, until Shiloh come; and unto him shall the gathering of the people be."[116]

In this translation Shiloh is interpreted as the Christ to whom the scepter or ruling power belongs.

Note that in the same passage in the Standard Hebrew Text, a different translation that was not subject to manipulation is stated:

> "The sceptre shall not depart from Judah, Nor the ruler's staff from between his feet, As long as men come to Shiloh; And unto him shall the obedience of the peoples be."[117]

While the precise meaning of Genesis 49:10 has been debated for generations the relatively unknown translation from the Standard Hebrew Text shows that no prophetic meaning was intended originally. That would be because the words "As long as men come to Shiloh" indicate those who were traveling to Shiloh on religious pilgrimages. Shiloh stopped being the location of the religious center long before the monarchal line of Judah began with David. The early translators and interpreters of Genesis 49:10 who proclaimed it to be prophetic did not want to draw attention to Shiloh as an earlier religious center and thereby draw attention away from Jerusalem. David proved it was not a prophecy by moving his religious center to Jerusalem. Also, the Christian interpreters were anxious to find any wording that could be used to show that the Christ figure was prophesied.

Judah had twin sons, Pharez and Zerah. At the time of their birth the midwife tied a red string around the wrist of the first hand that appeared during their births, in order to mark the firstborn. As soon as she had done that, though, the hand was withdrawn, and the other baby actually was born first. The baby with the red string was named Zerah, and his brother was named Pharez. Pharez received the rights inherent to the firstborn. It was from Pharez's line that David and Solomon and the successive kings of Judah emerged. Zerah eventually traveled away to establish his own line in exile. The line of Zerah continued on through the generations, but not in the land of Judah. His descendants continued to move on and many ultimately settled in Hibernia, which is now called Ireland. It was there that Oliolla lived.

Not long after Princess Tephi arrived in 583 B.C., her marriage to Oliolla was arranged. Princess Tephi, being the daughter of Zedekiah, was in the royal line of David descending from Judah's son Pharez. Oliolla was descended from Judah's son Zerah[118] through the direct descent line that included Milesius of Spain, his 12th great-grandfather, and perhaps the greatest warrior in all of history.

("Milesius … went with his Gadelians to Egypt, where he so signalized himself in the wars with the neighboring nations, that he was made general-in-chief by Pharaoh Nectanebus, who gave him his daughter Scota in marriage. After remaining seven years in Egypt, Milesius was reminded of the prophecy of Moses, which had been handed down, that the offspring of Gadelas should inhabit a large western island, and with sixty ships, his wife Scota and his people, set sail for Ireland; touched at Thrace; first landed in the kingdom of the Picts (now Scotland), and, finding the natives of Ireland too formidable, directed his course for the bay of Biscay, and finally landed in Spain; aided the Spaniards in expelling the Goths from their kingdom, and finally died in Spain, without ever setting foot in Ireland. After the death of Milesius, Scota and her sons, with a well appointed fleet and army, bearing on their standard a dead serpent and the rod of Moses, in memory of their ancestor Gadelas, set sail and landed in Ireland….After many hard fought battles, in one of which Scota was slain, the descendants of Gadelas possessed themselves of Ireland, as foretold by Moses …."[119])

The marriage of Princess Tephi and Oliolla would accomplish miraculous things. It would heal the breach between the two lines of Judah. The future monarchs who would descend from Oliolla and Princess Tephi would carry on the Davidic Bloodline and the Throne of David forever.[120] The transfer of power from the Pharez line of Judah to the Zerah line of Judah which resulted from their marriage would fulfill Ezekiel's prophecy.[121] In addition, Jeremiah's commission "to build, and to plant"[122] would be achieved by his having taken Zedekiah's daughter, Princess Tephi, safely to Hibernia and having overseen her marriage to Oliolla the Zerahite upon the sacred Stone of Destiny in 583 B.C.

As shown on pages 88 and 89 of this book the descendants of Oliolla and Princess Tephi, carrying the royal line of Judah, continued through the Irish kings, then the Scottish kings, and later to the monarchs of England.[123] Living descendants have direct ancestors who carried the Davidic Bloodline down to them, and after them, to all of their descendants; and those ancestors shared the royal line of Judah for over 2,100 years until their ancestral line reached Henry of Scotland, the son of David I, King of Scotland, and the grandson of Malcolm III of Scotland.[124]

The royal line of Queen Victoria and ultimately Queen Elizabeth II continued down to them through Henry's son, David, Earl of Huntingdon.[125] The line from Judah also continued down to modern times through Henry's son, William I, The Lion, King of Scotland, and through Henry's aunt, Matilda (Edith) of Scotland, the wife of Henry I, King of England.[126]

As shown on page 87 of this book the royal ancestors of Joseph of Arimathea and Jesus, descending from Judah, the son of Jacob, including David, Solomon, Hezekiah, and Josiah, came down through a granddaughter of King Josiah, Princess Tamar; and those ancestors were then shared with all of the subsequent, more recent, ancestors of Joseph of Arimathea and Jesus, and with all of the descendants of Joseph of Arimathea. Also, as shown on page 87, the priestly line from Levi, the son of Jacob, through Aaron and his son Eleazar connected with the royal line from David through Solomon by the marriage of Jerushah to Uzziah, resulting in all of their son's (Jotham's) descendants having both a priestly and a royal ancestral line.[127]

As shown on page 41 of this book, some descendants of Joseph of Arimathea, carrying the Davidic Bloodline, can be traced through Charlemagne and Isabel de Vermandois directly into modern times.[128]

RHN
AND
ELN

Section 9
A Genealogical Chart Showing a Descent Line From David, Through Solomon
(to Joseph of Arimathea and Jesus)
Researched by Robert H. Nelson and Emma L. Nelson

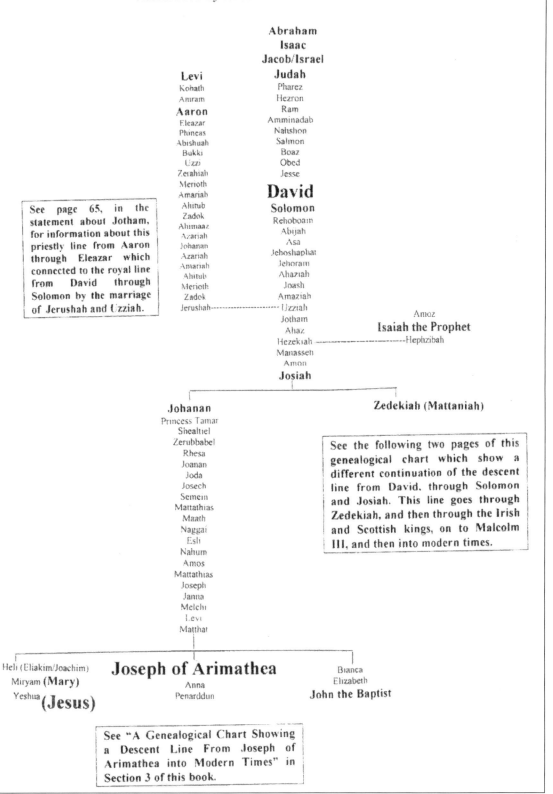

Abraham
Isaac
Jacob/Israel

Levi   **Judah**
Kohath   Pharez
Amram   Hezron
Aaron   Ram
Eleazar   Amminadab
Phineas   Nahshon
Abishuah   Salmon
Bukki   Boaz
Uzzi   Obed
Zerahiah   Jesse
Merioth
Amariah   **David**
Ahitub
Zadok   **Solomon**
Ahimaaz   Rehoboam
Azariah   Abijah
Johanan   Asa
Azariah   Jehoshaphat
Amariah   Jehoram
Ahitub   Ahaziah
Merioth   Joash
Zadok   Amaziah
Jerushah----------------Uzziah

See page 65, in the statement about Jotham, for information about this priestly line from Aaron through Eleazar which connected to the royal line from David through Solomon by the marriage of Jerushah and Uzziah.

Jotham
Ahaz   Amoz
            Isaiah the Prophet
Hezekiah --------------------Hephzibah
Manasseh
Amon
Josiah

Johanan   **Zedekiah (Mattaniah)**
Princess Tamar
Shealtiel
Zerubbabel
Rhesa
Joanan
Joda
Josech
Semein
Mattathias
Maath
Naggai
Esli
Nahum
Amos
Mattathias
Joseph
Janna
Melchi
Levi
Matthat

See the following two pages of this genealogical chart which show a different continuation of the descent line from David, through Solomon and Josiah. This line goes through Zedekiah, and then through the Irish and Scottish kings, on to Malcolm III, and then into modern times.

Heli (Eliakim/Joachim)   **Joseph of Arimathea**   Bianca
Miryam **(Mary)**   Anna   Elizabeth
Yeshua **(Jesus)**   Penarddun   **John the Baptist**

See "A Genealogical Chart Showing a Descent Line From Joseph of Arimathea into Modern Times" in Section 3 of this book.

Section 9
A Genealogical Chart Showing a Descent Line From David, Through Solomon (and Zedekiah to Malcolm III)
Researched by Robert H. Nelson and Emma L. Nelson

Zedekiah (Mattaniah)
Princess Tephi
Giallchadh
Nuahas Fionn Fail
Aodhain Glas
Simeon Breac
Muireadach Bolgrach
Fiachadh Tolgrach
Duach Laidrach
Eochaidh Buaigllorg
Ugaine Mor
Cobhthach Coalbreag
Meilage
Jaran Fathach
Conla Caomb
Olioll Caisfhiachach
Eochaidh Alethair
Aengus Tuirmheach Teamharch
Eana Aighneach
Labhra
Blathachtach
Eassmain Eamhna
Roighnein Ruadh
Fionnlog
Fionn
Eochaidh Feidhlioch
Fineamhuas
Lughaidh
Criomthan Niadhnar
Fearaidhach Fion-Feachtnuigh
Fiachadh Fionoluidh
Tuathal Teachtmar
Fedlimid Rachtmar
Coun Ceadchathach
Airt Aonthir
Cormac Ulfhota
Caibre Liffeachair
Fiachadh Sreabthuine
Muireadhach Tireach
Eochaid Moigmeodhin
Niall
Eogan
Muireadhach
Fergus Mor
Domangart
Gabran
Aidan
Eochaid
Domnall
Domangart
Eochaid
Eochaid
Aedh
Eochaid
Alpin
Kenneth I
Constantine I
Donald II
Malcolm I
Kenneth II
Malcolm II
Bethoc
Duncan I
Malcolm III of Scotland

Section 9
A Genealogical Chart Showing a Descent Line
From David, Through Solomon
(and Malcolm III into Modern Times)
Researched by Robert H. Nelson and Emma L. Nelson

Malcolm III of Scotland

David I, King of Scotland
Henry of Scotland
William I, The Lion, King of Scotland
Isabel of Scotland
William de Ros
William de Ros
Lucy de Ros
William de Plumpton
Alice de Plumpton
Margaret de Sherburne
Richard (de Bayley) de Sherburne
Richard Sherburne
Agnes Sherburne
Nicholas Rushton
Agnes Rushton
Peter Worthington
Isabel Worthington
Peter Worden
Eleanor Worden
John Adams
Sarah Adams
Susannah Cowperthwaite
Grace Webster
Hugh Shotwell
John Shotwell
Catherine Shotwell
John Shotwell Goe
Dorcas Rebecca Colvin Goe

Matilda (Edith) of Scotland
Matilda of England (the Empress)
Henry II, King of England
William Longespee
Stephen Longespee
Ela Longespee
Alan la Zouche
Maud la Zouche
Maud de Holland
Robert de Swynnerton
Maud de Swynnerton
Margaret Savage
Eleanor Dutton
Janet Langford
Alice Thelwall
John ap Harri Wynne
Rhys ap John Wynne
John ap Rhys Wynne
Thomas ap John Wynne
Dr. Thomas Wynne
Sydney Wynne
Anne Chew   Margaret Chew
Susannah Randall------Benjamin Brown
Richard Brown
Martha Patty Brown
Alpheus Gans
John Heaton Gans

The genealogical descent lines shown here illustrate the more recent ancestors of Dorcas Rebecca Colvin Goe (1849-1929) and John Heaton Gans (1849-1927) who both descended from David, through Solomon, and who married each other, combining their ancestors for succeeding generations.

The earlier line to Malcolm III separates into the lines of two of his children with his wife Margaret Atheling: David I, King of Scotland, and Matilda (Edith) of Scotland, the wife of Henry I, King of England.

Bertha Happy Gans
1879-1968

"Levi and Judah are glorified of the Lord
among the children of Jacob;
for God hath planted himself in them,
giving to the one the priesthood,
and to the other the kingdom ...."

The Testament of the Twelve Patriarchs, the Sons of Jacob

Notes for Part One: Joseph of Arimathea and Jesus

1. John 19:38 (King James Version)

2. James Edward Talmage, *Jesus the Christ* (Salt Lake City: The Deseret News, 1915), 35.

3. Nancy L. Kuehl, *Becoming Christian: The Demise of the Jesus Movement* (Eugene, Oregon: Resource Publications, 2014), 123.

4. Lionel Smithett Lewis, *St. Joseph of Arimathea at Glastonbury, or The Apostalic Church of Britain* (London: James Clarke & Co. Ltd., 1922), 157, 177.

5. Hannah Daviess Pittman, *Americans of Gentle Birth and Their Ancestors* (Baltimore: Genealogical Publishing Company, 1970), II: 27.

6. Lewis, *St. Joseph of Arimathea at Glastonbury*, 175.

7. *The Jewish Encyclopedia* (New York: Funk and Wagnalls, 1904), VII: 256.

8. *The Jewish Encyclopedia*, VII: 256.

9. Joseph Ratzinger (Pope Benedict XVI), *Jesus of Nazareth: From the Baptism in the Jordan to the Transfiguration* (New York: The Doubleday Broadway Publishing Group, 2007), 14.

10. *Encyclopedia Britannica* (Edinburgh: Archibald Constable and Company,1823), XVI: 251-252.

11. Randy DeMain, *The Nephilim Agenda* (Maricopa, Arizona: XP Publishing, 2010), 79.

12. Rev. Alexander McCaul, *The Old Paths, or A Comparison of the Principals and Doctrines of Modern Judaism with the Religion of Moses and the Prophets* (London: British Society for the Propagation of the Gospel, 1837), 63.

13. *Encyclopedia Britannica,* XVI: 252.

14. John 19:38

15. Detail from File:Heinrich Hoffman 3.png, commons.wikimedia.org

16. Matthew 27:57-60

17. Mark 15:43-46

18. Luke 23:50-53

19. John 19:38

20. Lewis, *St. Joseph of Arimathea at Glastonbury*, 175-176.

21. Lewis, *St. Joseph of Arimathea at Glastonbury*, 90.

22. Caesaris S. R. E. Card. Baroni, *Annales Ecclesiastici* (Parisiis: Barri-Ducis, MDCCCLXIV), I: 208. *(JESU CHRISTI ANNUS 35)*

23. Lady Anabel Kerr, *The Life of Cesare Cardinal Baronius* (London: Art and Book Company, 1898), 81.

24. R. W. Morgan, *St. Paul in Britain; or The Origin of British as Opposed to Papal Christianity* (London: The Covenant Publishing Co., 1900), 120.

25. John William Taylor, *The Coming of the Saints* (London: Methuen & Company, 1906), 126.

26. File: Maps-roman-empire-peak-150AD.jpg, commons.wikimedia.org

27. Taylor, *Coming of the Saints*, 179.

28. Lewis, *St. Joseph of Arimathea*, 93.

29. Morgan, *St. Paul in Britain*, 125.

30. Morgan, *St. Paul in Britain*, 125.

31. Matthew 10:5-6

32. Matthew 5-7

33. Andrew Gray, *The Origin and Early History of Christianity in Britain* (London: Skeffington & Sons, 1897), 12.

34. Acts 1:26

35. Lewis, *St. Joseph of Arimathea*, 111.

36. Lewis, *St. Joseph of Arimathea*, 94.

37. Lewis, *St. Joseph of Arimathea*, 94.

38. Morgan, *St. Paul in Britain,* 108.

39. Lewis, *St. Joseph of Arimathea*, 111.

40. Matthew 1:23

41. The Holy Scriptures According to the Masoretic Text (Philadelphia: The Jewish Publication Society of America, 1917), 487.

42. Robert Taylor, *The Diegesis; Being a Discovery of the Origins, Evidences, and Early History of Christianity* (Boston: J. P. Mendum, 1873), 265.

43. George Howard, trans., *Hebrew Gospel of Matthew* (Macon, Georgia: Mercer University Press, 1995), 5. (Matthew 1:23)

44. Numbers 23:19

45. Mark 12:29

46. Deuteronomy 6:14

47. 1 Chronicles 28:5-7

48. Matthew 1:11

49. Jeremiah 22:30

50. James Anderson, *Royal Genealogies, or the Genealogical Tables of Emperors, Kings, and Princes* (London: James Bettenham, 1732), 308.

51. Lewis, *St. Joseph of Arimathea*, 68, 90.

52. *The Encyclopedia Americana* (New York: The Encyclopedia Americana Corporation, 1919), 346.

53. Lewis, *St. Joseph of Arimathea,* 68.

54. Detail from File:Leonardo de Vinci - Vierge, Enfant Jesus, ste Anne & st Jean - Baptiste 1.jpg, commons.wikimedia.org

55. *Munificentissimus Deus* was an "infallible" statement made by Pope Pius XII on November 1, 1950 regarding the Assumption of Mary.

56. *Munificentissimus Deus* became a binding teaching, meaning that those Catholics who disagree with it are no longer considered to be Catholics by the Roman Catholic Church, and are essentially excommunicated from the Church.

57. Acts 1:14

58. Lewis, *St. Joseph of Arimathea,* 68, 90, 169-171.

59. Romans 7:19

60. Matthew 7:15

61. Matthew 5:19

62. Acts 21:28

63. Romans 16:11

64. *British Museum Catalogue of Printed Books: A-A* (London: William Clowes and Sons, Limited, 1886), Dole-Doughty, 202.

65. Taylor, *The Diegesis,* 262, 265.

66. Arthur Dyott Thomson, *The Gospel History and Doctrinal Teaching Critically Examined* (London: Longmans, Green, and Co., 1873), 193.

67. Taylor, *The Diegesis,* 283.

68. Thomson, *The Gospel History,* 193.

69. Taylor, *The Diegesis,* 262, 265.

70. Alexander Roberts and James Donaldson, eds., *Ante-Nicene Christian Library: Translations of the Writings of the Fathers Down to A.D. 325* (Edinburgh: T. and T. Clark, 1867), III (Writings of Tatian, Theophilus; and the Clementine Recognitions), 188.

71. Mark 6:3

72. Luke 23:27

73. Matthew 27:56

74. Mark 15:40

75. John 19:25

76. Detail from File:Heinrich Hoffman 3.png, commons.wikimedia.org

77. Mark 15:40, John 19:25

78. R. B. Paul, *Short Notes of the Four Gospels* (Oxford: J. Vincent, 1829), 16.

79. Benjamin H. Freedman, *Facts Are Facts* (Carson City, Nevada: Bridger House Publishers, Inc., 2009), 15, 21.

80. Genesis 32:28

81. Isaiah 41:8

82. 2 Kings 16:6

83. Genesis 36:8-9

84. *The Banner of Israel* (London: W. H. Guest, 1881), V: 267.

85. *The Jewish Encyclopedia*, III: 629.

86. Genesis 36:8-9

87. *The Jewish Encyclopedia*, X: 284.

88. 1 Kings 11:3-5

89. David Einsiedler, "Can We Prove Descent from King David?," *Online Journal,* jewishgen.org

90. Bernhard Pick, *Jesus in the Talmud* (London: The Open Court Publishing Company, 1913), 13-44.

91. Martin Luther, *Von den Juden und ihren Lügen* (Wittenberg, 1543)

92. Martin Luther, *On the Jews and Their Lies* (Uckfield, England: The Historical Review Press, 2011), 4.

93. David Turner, "Jewish Problem Sources, the Gospels: 'You are of your father, the devil.'" jpost.com/blogs, 9/20/2014.

94. John 8:44

95. Genesis 12:3

96. Charles H. Hoole, trans., *The Didache or Teaching of the Twelve Apostles* (London: David Nutt, 1894), 25-85.

97. John 10:16

98. Hosea 1:11

99. Matthew 28:19-20

100. Matthew 10:5-6

101. Matthew 15:24

102. James Orr, ed., *The International Standard Bible Encyclopedia* (Chicago: Howard-Severance Company, 1915), IV: 2637.

103. *British Museum Catalogue,* Dole-Doughty, 202.

104. Taylor, *The Diegesis,* 262, 265.

105. David Noel Freedman, *Eerdmans Dictionary of the Bible* (Grand Rapids: Wm. B. Eerdmans Publishing Co., 2000), 874.

106. Lynn Lundquist, *The Tetragrammation and the Christian Greek Scriptures* (Grand Rapids: Word Resources, Inc., 1998), Chapter 5: "Matthew's Gospel in Hebrew."

107. Howard, *Hebrew Gospel of Matthew,* 151. (Matthew 28:19-20)

108. Mark 16:15-16

109. *Codex Sinaiticus* and *Codex Vaticanus*

110. Anderson, *Royal Genealogies,* 310-312.

111. Genesis 32:28

112. Luke 3:24-34

113. *Dictionary of the Bible* (New York: Eaton & Mains, 1900), 550.

114. 1 Chronicles 16:13

115. Roger Rusk, *The Other End of the World*: *An Alternate Theory Linking Prophecy and History* (Plano, Texas: Le Book Company, Inc., 1988), 182.

116. Moses Mielziner, *Introduction to the Talmud* (London: Funk & Wagnalls Company, 1903), 110.

117. George Holly Gilbert, *Jesus* (New York: The Macmillan Company, 1912), 193.

118. Matthew 15:1-3

119. File:Brooklyn Museum - The Pharisees Question Jesus - James Tissot.jpg, commons.wikimedia.org

120. James Stalker, *The Christology of Jesus* (London: Hodder & Stoughton, 1899), 144.

121. Rusk, *The Other End of the World,* 182.

122. Malachi 1:2-3

123. Genesis 36:8-9

124. Matthew 15:24

125. Matthew 10:5-6

126. John 10:26-27

127. Isaiah 41:8

128. Genesis 36:8-9

129. Shlomo Sand, *The Invention of the Jewish People* (London: Verso, 2009), 158.

130. McCaul, *The Old Paths,* 63.

131. John 8:31-33

132. Exodus 1:11-14

133. Sand, *The Invention of the Jewish People*, 158.

134. Anderson, *Royal Genealogies*, 310-312.

135. Anderson, *Royal Genealogies*, 308.

136. DeMain, *The Nephilim Agenda,* 79.

137. Freedman, *Facts Are Facts*, 26.

138. Freedman, *Facts Are Facts*, 24-25.

Notes for Part Two: The Priestly Ancestry

1. *The Testament of the Twelve Patriarchs, The Sons of Jacob* (London: James, Joseph, and Isaac Frost, 1837), 43.

2. Luke 1:34-37 (King James Version)

3. James Anderson, *Royal Genealogies, or the Genealogical Tables of Emperors, Kings, and Princes* (London: James Bettenham, 1732), 311-312.

4. Luke 3:25-31

5. Hebrews 7:14

6. *Calmet's Dictionary of the Holy Bible* (Boston: Crocker and Brewster, 1832), 855.

7. Exodus 28:1

8. Exodus 28:43

9. Leviticus 10:1-2

10. Numbers 20:27-29

11. Numbers 25:1-3

12. Numbers 25:7-8

13. 1 Chronicles 6:3-4

14. 1 Chronicles 6:3-5

15. File:PLATE4DX.jpg, commons.wikimedia.org

16. 1 Chronicles 6:3-5

17. 1 Chronicles 6:3-8

18. Gilbert Burrington, *An Arrangement of the Genealogies in the Old Testament* (London: C. & J. Rivington and W. Strong, 1836), I: 106-107.

19. 1 Kings 1:39-46

20. 1 Chronicles 6:3-8

21. 1 Chronicles 6:3-9

22. 1 Chronicles 6:13

23. 2 Chronicles 34:14-16

24. 1 Chronicles 6:13

25. 1 Chronicles 6:14

26. Jeremiah 52:24-27

27. 1 Chronicles 6:14

28. Ezra 3:2

29. Nehemiah 12:10

30. Nehemiah 12:10

31. Nehemiah 13:4-9

32. Nehemiah 12:10

33. 2 Kings 11:1-16

34. Nehemiah 12:11

35. Nehemiah 12:11

36. Burrington, *An Arrangement of Genealogies in the Old Testament,* Table X - No. 2.

37. John Platts, *A New Universal Biography* (London: Sherwood, Jones, and Co., 1825), I: 502.

38. Charles Carroll Everett et al., eds., *The New World* (Boston: Houghton, Mifflin, and Company, 1892), I: 113.

39. Platts, *A New Universal Biography,* I: 502.

40. Everett, *The New World*, I: 113.

41. Anderson, *Royal Genealogies*, 310.

42. Anderson, *Royal Genealogies*, 312.

43. Hebrews 7:14

44. Hebrews 5:6

45. Exodus 40:15

46. Bible Cyclopedia (London: John W. Parker, 1841), I: 1.

47. Exodus 2:1-10

48. *The Jewish Encyclopedia* (New York: Funk and Wagnalls, 1904), I: 2.

49. T. G. Beharrell, *Biblical Biography* (Indianapolis: Downey & Browse, 1867), 9.

50. Exodus 4:27

51. Beharrell, *Biblical Biography,* 9.

52. Exodus 4:29-31

53. Exodus 7:7

54. Exodus 14:26-30

55. Exodus 25:31-32

56. Exodus 28:1

57. Exodus 28:43

58. Beharrell, *Biblical Biography*, 10.

59. Detail from File:Holman Consecration of Aaron and His Sons.jpg, commons.wikimedia.org

60. Numbers 16:28-32

61. Numbers 17:1-8

62. Numbers 20:27-29

63. Beharrell, *Biblical Biography*, 11-12.

Notes for Part Three: The Royal Ancestry

1. *The Testament of the Twelve Patriarchs, The Sons of Jacob* (London: James, Joseph, and Isaac Frost, 1837), 70.

2. G. H. Eliason, *The Generations of Antichrist: An Argument for the Sake of Heaven* (Denver: Outskirts Press, 2011), 83-84.

3. A. R. Fausset, *Bible Cyclopaedia, Critical and Expository* (Hartford: The S. S. Scranton Company, 1905), 736.

4. 1 Kings 11:42 (King James Version)

5. 2 Chronicles 5:1-2

6. Proverbs 1-29

7. 1 Kings 11:4-5

8. File:Solomon oversees the construction of the temple.jpg, commons.wikimedia.org

9. 1 Kings 14:31

10. 1 Kings 14:21

11. James Augustus Hessey, *Biographies of the Kings of Judah, Twelve Lectures* (London: Rivingtons, Waterloo Place, 1865), 20-21.

12. 1 Kings 15:2

13. I Kings 15:10

14. Hessey, *Biographies of the Kings of Judah,* 21.

15. 2 Chronicles 20:31-32

16. 2 Chronicles 17:4-5

17. 2 Kings 8:16-17

18. 2 Chronicles 22:11

19. Hessey, *Biographies of the Kings of Judah,* 61.

20. 2 Kings 8:18

21. 2 Kings 8:26

22. 2 Kings 11:1-3

23. 2 Kings 12:1

24. 2 Kings 11:4-16

25. 2 Kings 12:2

26. 2 Kings 12:20

27. 2 Chronicles 25:1

28. 2 Chronicles 25:3

29. 2 Chronicles 25:2

30. 2 Chronicles 25:27

31. 2 Chronicles 26:3

32. 2 Chronicles 26

33. 2 Chronicles 26:4

34. 2 Chronicles 26:18

35. 2 Chronicles 27:1

36. John Platts, *A New Universal Biography* (London: Sherwood, Jones, and Co., 1825), I: 173.

37. 2 Chronicles 27:6

38. Hessey, *Biographies of the Kings of Judah,* 127.

39. 2 Kings 16:18

40. 2 Chronicles 29:1

41. 2 Kings 21:1

42. 2 Chronicles 32:33

43. 2 Kings 21:1

44. Hessey, *Biographies of the Kings of Judah*, 165.

45. 2 Kings 21:19

46. Hessey, *Biographies of the Kings of Judah*, 182.

47. 2 Kings 21:23

48. File:Josias rex.jpg, commons.wikimedia.org

49. 2 Kings 22:1

50. 2 Chronicles 34:3

51. 2 Chronicles 34:14-32

52. Platts, *A New Universal Biography*, I: 204.

53. 2 Chronicles 34:33

54. 2 Chronicles 35:24-25

55. William Whiston, trans., *The Works of Flavius Josephus* (Edinburgh: University Press, 1830), 272.

56. *Calmet's Great Dictionary of the Holy Bible* (Charlestown: Samuel Etheridge, Jun., 1813), II (found in entry on "Manasseh, fifteenth king of Judah").

57. Luke 4:16-20

58. Isaiah 61:1-2

59. *A Dictionary of the Bible* (New York: Charles Scribner's Sons, 1911), 487.

60. Luke 3:32-34

61. 1 Chronicles 10:13-14

62. 1 Samuel 16:1-13

63. 1 Samuel 17:34-35

64. William M. Taylor, *David, King of Israel: His Life and Its Lessons* (New York: Harper and Brothers, Publishers, 1875), 15.

65. 1 Samuel 16:19-23

66. 1 Samuel 17:17-40

67. 1 Samuel 17:41-54

68. File:071A.David Slays Goliath.jpg, commons.wikimedia.org

69. 1 Samuel 19:11-17

70. 1 Samuel 20:18-42

71. 1 Samuel 21:1-9

72. 1 Samuel 22:18-19

73. 1 Samuel 21:10-15

74. 1 Samuel 22:20-23

75. 1 Samuel 23:5

76. 1 Samuel 23:16-18

77. 1 Samuel 24:2-22

78. 1 Samuel 26:5-25

79. 1 Samuel 25:1-42

80. 1 Samuel 27:3-12

81. 1 Samuel 30

82. 1 Samuel 31

83. 1 Chronicles 12:1-22

84. 2 Samuel 3:1

85. 2 Samuel 3:14-16

86. 2 Samuel 3:26-39

87. 2 Samuel 4

88. 2 Samuel 5:11

89. 2 Samuel 6

90. 2 Samuel 7:12-13

91. 2 Samuel 9

92. 2 Samuel 11

93. 2 Samuel 12:7-14

94. 2 Samuel 18:33

95. File:Study of King David, by Julia Margaret Cameron.jpg, commons.wikimedia.org

96. 1 Kings 1:5

97. 1 Kings 1:11-53

98. 1 Kings 2:11

99. Robert H. and Emma L. Nelson, *From Great Men: The Famous Ancestors of Alice de Plumpton* (Denver: Outskirts Press, 2012), 123.

100. The Holy Scriptures According to the Masoretic Text (Philadelphia: The Jewish Publication Society of America, 1917), 791.

101. 2 Samuel 7:16

102. Jeremiah 52:1

103. Jeremiah 1:1

104. Jeremiah 16:1-2

105. Jeremiah 52:10-11

106. Jeremiah 1:9-10

107. File:123.Baruch Writes Jeremiah's Prophesies.jpg, commons.wikimedia.org

108. Jeremiah 43:6-7

109. Isaiah 37:31-32

110. Genesis 28:10-22

111. Jeremiah 3:16

112. Jeremiah 3:16

113. Dermod O'Connor, trans., *Keating's General History of Ireland* (Dublin: James Duffy, Sons, & Co., 1865), 171-172.

114. Mary Beecher Longyear, *Hear, O Israel!* (Boston: Press of Geo H. Ellis Co. 1922), 16.

115. Deuteronomy 33:7

116. Genesis 49:10

117. The Holy Scriptures According to the Masoretic Text, 62. (Genesis 49:10)

118. Charles Adiel Lewis Totten, *The Romance of History* (New Haven: Our Race Pub. Co., 1891), 200.

119. *The New England Historical and Genealogical Register* (New England Historic Genealogical Society, 1869), XXIII: 125.

120. 2 Samuel 7:16

121. Ezekiel 17:24

122. Jeremiah 1:9-10

123. Annah Robinson Watson, *A Royal Lineage: Alfred the Great, 901-1901* (Richmond: Whittet & Shepperson, 1901), 20-21.

124. See Section 9: "A Genealogical Chart Showing a Descent Line From David, Through Solomon (and Zedekiah to Malcolm III) (and Malcolm III into Modern Times)."

125. George Russell French, *The Ancestry of Her Majesty Queen Victoria, and of His Royal Highness Prince Albert* (London: William Pickering, 1841), 195.

126. See Section 9: "A Genealogical Chart Showing a Descent Line From David, Through Solomon (and Zedekiah to Malcolm III) (and Malcolm III into Modern Times)."

127. 2 Chronicles 26:23, 2 Chronicles 27:1

128. See Section 3: "A Genealogical Chart Showing a Descent Line From Joseph of Arimathea into Modern Times."

Anderson, James. *Royal Genealogies, Or the Genealogical Tables of Emperors, Kings and Princes.* London: James Bettenham, 1732.

Baronii, Caesaris S.R.E. Card. *Annales Ecclesiastici.* Parisiis: Barri-Ducis, MDCCCLXIV.

Burrington, Gilbert. *An Arrangement of the Genealogies in the Old Testament.* London: C. & J. Rivington and W. Strong, 1836.

Encyclopaedia Britannica (Eleventh Edition). New York: The Encyclopaedia Britannica Company, 1910.

Fowler, Henry Thatcher. *The Origin and Growth of the Hebrew Religion.* Chicago: The University of Chicago Press, 1916.

Freedman, Benjamin H. *Facts Are Facts.* Carson City, Nevada: Bridger House Publishers, Inc., 2009.

Garretson, Arthur Samuel. *Primitive Christianity and Early Criticisms.* Boston: Sherman, French & Company, 1912.

Gray, Andrew. *The Origin and Early History of Christianity in Britain.* London: Skeffington & Son, 1897.

Harper, William Rainey. *The Priestly Element in The Old Testament.* Chicago: The University of Chicago Press, 1905.

Hessey, James Augustus. *Biographies of the Kings of Judah.* London: Rivingtons, 1865.

The Holy Bible Containing the Old and New Testaments (King James Version). Glasgow: William Collins, Sons and Company, 1839.

The Holy Scriptures According to the Masoretic Text. Philadelphia: The Jewish Publication Society of America, 1917.

Hoole, Charles H., trans. *The Didache or Teaching of the Twelve Apostles.* London: David Nutt, 1894.

Howard, George, trans. *Hebrew Gospel of Matthew.* Macon, Georgia: Mercer University Press, 1995.

The International Standard Bible Encyclopaedia. Chicago: The Howard-Severance Company, 1915.

Lewis, Abram Herbert. *Paganism Surviving in Christianity.* New York: G. P. Putnam's Sons, 1892.

Lewis, Lionel Smithett. *St. Joseph of Arimathea at Glastonbury.* London: A.R. Mowbray, 1922.

Selected Bibliography

Marti, Karl. *The Religion of the Old Testament.* London: Williams & Norgate, 1907.

Milner, The Rev. W. M. H. *The Royal House of Britain: An Enduring Dynasty.* London: The Covenant Publishing Co., 1991.

Milroy, Adam, trans. *The Prophets and Prophecy in Israel.* London: Longmans, Green and Co., 1877.

Morgan, R. W. *St. Paul in Britain; or, The Origin of British as Opposed to Papal Christianity.* London: The Covenant Publishing Co., 1900.

Nelson, Robert H. and Emma L. *From Great Men: The Famous Ancestors of Alice de Plumpton.* (eBook edition) Austin: Robert H. Nelson, 2012. (print edition) Denver: Outskirts Press, 2012.

O'Connor, Dermod, trans. (Geoffrey) *Keating's General History of Ireland.* Dublin: James Duffy, Sons, & Co., 1865.

O'Hart, John. *Irish Pedigrees; Or, The Origin and Stem of The Irish Nation.* Dublin: M. H. Gill & Son, 1881.

Sanders, Frank Knight. *History of the Hebrews.* New York: Charles Scribner's Sons, 1914.

Schweitzer, Albert. *The Quest of the Historical Jesus.* London: Adam and Charles Black, 1910.

Stalker, James. *The Christology of Jesus.* London: Hodder & Stoughton, 1899.

Taylor, John William. *The Coming of the Saints.* London: Methuen & Company, 1906.

Taylor, Robert. *The Diegesis; Being a Discovery of the Origin, Evidences, and Early History of Christianity.* London: R. Carlile, 1829.

Taylor, William M. *David, King of Israel.* New York: Harper & Brothers, Publishers, 1875.

The Testament of the Twelve Patriarchs, the Sons of Jacob. London: James, Joseph, and Isaac Frost, 1837.

Tregelles, Samuel P. *On the Original Language of St. Matthew's Gospel.* London: Samuel Bagster and Sons, 1850.

Whiston, William, trans. *The Works of Flavius Josephus.* Philadelphia: Jas. B. Smith & Co., 1854.

Wikimedia Commons, an online repository of free-use images. (commons.wikimedia.org)

Index

Index

Also Written by Robert H. Nelson and Emma L. Nelson

James M. Corns:
The Ancestry and Life of a Warrior

From Great Men:
The Famous Ancestors of Alice de Plumpton

Frederick Hill:
The Life and Lessons of a Patriot
for Children and Adults

Made in the USA
Lexington, KY
19 September 2015